Amazing Jingtai
魅力景泰

刘志昊 / 著

兰州大学出版社
LANZHOU UNIVERSITY PRESS

图书在版编目（CIP）数据

魅力景泰 = Amazing Jingtai : 汉英对照 / 刘志昊
著. -- 兰州 : 兰州大学出版社, 2025. 4. -- ISBN 978-
7-311-06892-9

Ⅰ. K924.24
中国国家版本馆 CIP 数据核字第 20257TG070 号

责任编辑　武素珍
封面设计　汪如祥

书　　名	Amazing Jingtai	
	魅力景泰	
作　　者	刘志昊　著	
出版发行	兰州大学出版社　（地址:兰州市天水南路222号　730000）	
电　　话	0931-8912613(总编办公室)　0931-8617156(营销中心)	
网　　址	http://press.lzu.edu.cn	
电子信箱	press@lzu.edu.cn	
印　　刷	陕西龙山海天艺术印务有限公司	
开　　本	710 mm×1020 mm　1/16	
成品尺寸	170 mm×240 mm	
印　　张	10.25	
字　　数	144千	
版　　次	2025年4月第1版	
印　　次	2025年4月第1次印刷	
书　　号	ISBN 978-7-311-06892-9	
定　　价	47.00元	

（图书若有破损、缺页、掉页，可随时与本社联系）

Preface

Located in central Gansu Province, the upper reaches of the Yellow River and the transitional zone between the Loess Plateau and the Tengger Desert, Jingtai, like a bright pearl embedded in the northwest of China, covers an area of 5,485 square kilometers and has a rich history spanning over 4,500 years. It's a key production base for commodity grain in China and an important industrial base in Gansu Province. It's also home to numerous historical relics and diverse natural landscapes like majestic mountains, spectacular canyons, lush forests, vast grasslands, magnificent wetlands, boundless Gobi desert, the beautiful Yellow River and the winding Great Wall.

This is the first English book that introduces Jingtai in a comprehensive and systematic manner. The main purpose is to show a more prosperous, more influential, more charming and more vibrant Jingtai, promote the brilliant culture, enhance cultural confidence and spread the voice of Jingtai. The content is in a bilingual format, featuring both English and Chinese. It's composed of 13 parts, including history, administrative division, geographical environment, population, natural resources, transportation, education and health care, folk culture, tourist attractions, special agricultural products, a taste of Jingtai, Jingtaichuan Electric Pumping Irrigation Project, and towns and townships of Jingtai.

My sincere gratitude goes to Cui Xiuzhong, Catherine H A Seda, Luo Chongzhong and Wei Lierong for their invaluable contributions to the book. They have helped in ways too numerous to recount. I am grateful as well to the Photographers Association of Jingtai for providing all the pictures in the book.

Due to limited time and knowledge, there may be unavoidably mistakes and drawbacks in the book. Your suggestions would be highly appreciated.

前　言

　　景泰县地处甘肃省中部、黄河上游、黄土高原与腾格里沙漠过渡地带，是镶嵌在中国西北部的一颗明珠。这里拥有5400多平方千米的广袤土地，承载着4500多年的厚重历史，是中国重点商品粮生产基地，也是甘肃省重要工业基地。在这片神奇的土地上，历史遗迹星罗棋布，自然风光绚丽多彩。高山、峡谷、森林、草原、湿地、戈壁沙漠、黄河、长城等景观交相辉映，共同绘就了一幅壮丽的画卷。

　　为展现一个更加繁荣、更具实力、更富魅力、更显活力的景泰，弘扬景泰璀璨文化，增强文化自信，向世界传播景泰声音，编者精心编写了首部全面展现景泰风貌的英文书籍。本书采用英汉双语对照的编写方式，共分十三章系统而全面地介绍了景泰的悠久历史、行政区划、地理环境、人口、自然资源、交通运输、教育医疗、民俗文化、旅游景点、特色农产品、景泰美食、景泰川电力提灌工程以及各个乡镇的独特风貌。

　　在本书的编写过程中，崔秀忠先生、Catherine H A Seda女士、罗崇忠先生和魏烈荣先生给予了无私的帮助和支持，在此，向他们致以最诚挚的谢意。同时，衷心感谢景泰县摄影家协会为本书提供了所有照片。

　　由于编写时间紧迫且编者水平有限，本书难免存在一些错误或不足之处，诚请批评指正。

Contents

Amazing Jingtai
魅力景泰

Located in the western part of China and on the southern fringe of the Tengger Desert, Jingtai covers an area of 5,485 square kilometers. Its land is shaped like a fluttering butterfly with a distance of around 84 kilometers from east to west and 102 kilometers from north to south. The terrain slopes from the southwest to the northeast, with an average altitude of 1,610 meters. Jingtai experiences hot summers and cold winters, with little rainfall but abundant sunlight. The temperature varies greatly between day and night.

Jingtai boasts a long history and rich culture. Archaeological findings at Zhangjiatai Ruins suggest that humans already labored, lived and multiplied on this land 4,500 years ago. In 67 BC, the region was set as Aowei County with Diaogou as the seat, marking the beginning of its history as a county. In 1913, it was established as Hongshui County with Kuangou as its seat, the second time the region had been set as a county in history. In 1933, the area was established as a county for the third time and named Jingtai County, which literally means "prosperity and peace". The county seat was initially located in Luyang but was relocated to Yitiaoshan in 1978.

Jingtai is a key production base for commodity grain in China and an important industrial base in Gansu Province. It's also well-known as a popular tourist destination and a film shooting base in northwestern China. The county has 8 towns (Yitiaoshan, Luyang, Xiquan, Caowotan, Hongshui, Zhenglu, Zhongquan, Shangshawo) and 3 townships (Wufo, Sitan, Manshuitan) under its administration. It's home to 25 ethnic groups living in harmony, with a population of 237,191 as of 2024.

景泰县地处中国西部,腾格里沙漠南缘,总面积5485平方千米。景泰县的轮廓宛若一只翩翩起舞的蝴蝶,东西长约84千米,南北宽约102千米,地势西南高,东北低,平均海拔1610米。这里冬冷夏热、干旱少雨、光照充足、昼夜温差大。

景泰县历史悠久、文化底蕴深厚。张家台遗址出土的文物表明,早在4500多年前,景泰先民就在这片土地上辛勤劳作、繁衍生息。公元前67年,景泰首次立县,名为媪围县,县城位于吊沟;1913年第二次立县,名为红水县,县城位于宽沟;1933年第三次立县,更名为景泰县,寓意"景象繁荣、国泰民安",县城起初设在芦阳,后于1978年迁至一条山镇。

景泰县是中国重点商品粮生产基地和甘肃省重要工业基地,也是中国西北著名的旅游胜地和影视拍摄基地。景泰县下辖8个镇和3个乡,包括一条山镇、芦阳镇、喜泉镇、草窝滩镇、红水镇、正路镇、中泉镇、上沙沃镇,以及五佛乡、寺滩乡、漫水滩乡。2024年景泰县总人口达到237191人,汇聚了25个民族,共同构成了一幅多元文化的绚丽画卷。

1

History 悠久历史

1.1 Brief History 历史沿革

The history of Jingtai can be traced back to the Neolithic Age, with archaeological evidence suggesting that human settlement in the region began more than 4,500 years ago.

During the Spring and Autumn Period (770 BC–476 BC), the area was inhabited by the Rong people. In the Warring States Period (475 BC–221 BC) and the Qin Dynasty (221 BC–207 BC), it was ruled by Yuezhi. When Yuezhi was defeated by the Huns in the early Han Dynasty (202 BC–220 AD), the region became part of King Xiuchu's territory until 121 BC, when Emperor Wu of Han established four prefectures in the Hexi Corridor and it came under the governance of the Han government. The area was set as Aowei County with Diaogou as its seat in 67 BC, marking the beginning of its history as a county.

During the Tang Dynasty (618-907), the region was controlled by Tubo for 86 years from the second year of Guangde Period (764) to the third year of Dazhong Period (849). In the Song Dynasty (960-1276), Western Xia, a kingdom founded by the Tangut ethnic group in the 11th century, established its rule over the area. During the Wanli Period of the Ming Dynasty, the area was once occupied by the Tartars but was recaptured by the Ming government in the 26th year of Wanli (1598).

During the Qing Dynasty (1616-1912), the region was designated as Hongshui Subcounty in the 22nd year of Emperor Qianlong (1757). In the second year of the Republic of China (1913), it was established as Hongshui County, with Kuangou as its seat. This was the second time the region had been set as a county.

In the 22nd year of the Republic of China (1933), the area was set as a county for the third time and named Jingtai County. The name "Jingtai" literally means "prosperity and peace". The seat was initially located in Luyang but was relocated to Yitiaoshan in 1978. Since then, it has gradually developed into a modern county.

早在4500多年前，景泰这片古老的土地上已有人类繁衍生息。

春秋时期，这里为戎族聚居之地。战国至秦时，属月氏属地。汉初，匈奴破月氏，此地遂成为匈奴休屠王的领地。汉武帝元狩二年（公元前121年），汉朝开辟河西走廊，设立四郡，景泰正式纳入汉朝版图。汉宣帝地节三年（公元前67年），在此设立媼围县，县治位于今吊沟古城，标志着景泰立县之始。

唐朝广德、大中年间，景泰被吐蕃控制。宋朝时，隶属于西夏。明朝万历年间，这里一度被鞑靼所据，至万历二十六年（1598），复归明朝版图。

清乾隆二十二年（1757），在此设红水分县。民国二年（1913），这里第二次立县，名为红水县，县城位于宽沟。

民国二十二年（1933），第三次立县，更名为景泰县，寓意"景象繁荣、国泰民安"。县城起初设在芦阳，1978年迁至一条山，开启了景泰发展史上的崭新篇章。

1.2 Aowei Site媪围古城遗址

Located approximately 5 kilometers east of Luyang, Aowei Site covers an area of around 460 *mu*, with a circumference of about 2,400 meters. It's the largest county-level site of Han Dynasty along the ancient Silk Road.

Built between 121 BC and 110 BC, Aowei, under the jurisdiction of Wuwei which was one of the four prefectures in the Hexi Corridor during the Han Dynasty, was the first major town on the Silk Road leading to the Western Regions. Jingtai County Annals recorded that "during the Western Han Dynasty, the Eastern Han Dynasty and the Three Kingdoms Period, Aowei enjoyed social stability and economic prosperity, and Buddhism became increasingly prevalent in the region during the Western Jin Dynasty and the Southern and Northern Dynasties". Both the farming and the commerce blossomed in ancient times, and the residents lived in peace and contentment. The relics unearthed from the Han Tombs of Xicun, Diaogouliang and Chengbeidun, such as pottery pieces, Han bricks and ancient coins, offer a glimpse into the region's past prosperity.

Aowei was not only a key customs pass and trading center but also an important fortress on the ancient Silk Road. The Great Wall was built in this area during the Wanli Period of the Ming Dynasty to defend against the nomadic invaders from the north. Today, there are still many mysteries about Aowei that remain to be explored.

媪围古城遗址位于芦阳镇向东约5千米处，周长约2400米，总面积约460亩，是丝绸之路沿线规模最大的汉代县城遗址。

　　媪围古城建于公元前121年至公元前110年之间，是丝绸之路通往西域的第一个重镇，隶属于"河西四郡"之一的武威郡。《景泰县志》记载，"西汉始，东汉、三国时，媪围境内安定富庶，西晋南北朝时期佛教日益盛行"。古时，这里人民生活安定、农业经济繁荣。西村汉墓、吊沟梁汉墓、城北敦汉墓出土的陶片、汉砖和古币等展现了当时这里的繁荣与辉煌。

　　媪围古城曾经是古丝绸之路上的重要通道和贸易中心，同时也是一座重要的军事堡垒。万历年间明朝政府在这一区域修筑长城，以加强边防。如今，媪围古城仍然有诸多谜团尚未被揭开。

Aowei Site

1.3 Zhangjiatai Ruins 张家台遗址

Zhangjiatai Ruins are located in Luyang, extending to Mowan on the east, Mahaodigou on the west, hills on the south and Zhangjiatai Tree Farm on the north. The ruins are distributed over a thin strip of land nearly 1,200 meters long from east to west and 100 meters wide from north to south.

Zhangjiatai Ruins were discovered accidentally by local villagers in 1969 and were identified as a site of the Majiayao Culture of the Neolithic Age in 1971. In 1975, an archaeological team from the Gansu Provincial Institute of Cultural Relics and Archaeology conducted excavations here, uncovering over 20 tombs and unearthing a great many invaluable relics, including painted pottery, red pottery, gray pottery, as well as stone knives, stone axes, bone knives and bone beads. These findings are crucial for studying the development of ancient Chinese civilization and have drawn high attention from archaeologists.

The discovery of Zhangjiatai Ruins has not only improved the understanding of the Majiayao Culture of the Neolithic Age, but also provided tangible evidence for the study of ancient lifestyles, pottery-making techniques and burial customs.

A Pottery Unearthed from Zhangjiatai Ruins

张家台遗址位于芦阳镇，东到磨湾村，西至马号地沟，南依丘陵，北接张家台村林场，分布在东西长约1200米、南北宽约100米的狭长地带。

张家台遗址1969年被当地村民偶然发现；1971年被认定为新石器时代马家窑文化的文化遗存，并受到保护；1975年由甘肃省考古队进行考古发掘，共清理墓葬20多座，出土彩陶、红陶、灰陶以及石刀、石斧、骨刀、骨珠等多件文物。这些文物是研究中国古代文明发展的重要资料，引起了考古界的高度重视。

张家台遗址的发现不仅丰富了人们对新石器时代马家窑文化的认识，也为研究古代人类的生活方式、制陶技术和埋葬习俗提供了实物证据。

1.4 Jingtai Rock Paintings 景泰岩画

Located in the upper reaches of the Yellow River and the intersection of Gansu Province, Ningxia Hui Autonomous Region and Inner Mongolia Autonomous Region, Jingtai, with its unique advantages in location and natural resources, was historically inhabited by nomads, who left behind a wealth of cultural heritage.

With a large number of rock paintings dating back to the Neolithic Age found in Sitan, Zhongquan, Hongshui, Zhenglu and Shangshawo, Jingtai is seen as one of the representative areas of rock paintings in northern China. The vivid images were carved on rock surfaces by ancient nomads and feature a wide range of subjects, including human figures and various animals like sheep, horses and deer. They mainly depict hunting scenes and sacrificial rites.

These rock paintings, considered as an "art history engraved on stones", are of great value and significance in the study of history, archaeology and art. They not only reflect the region's ecological environment in the remote past, but also provide valuable insights into the daily lives, religious beliefs and aesthetic preferences of the northern nomadic people.

景泰县地处黄河上游，位于甘肃、宁夏、内蒙古三省（区）交界处，由于特定的地理位置和丰富的自然资源，这里古时是草原牧民生活的家园，也因此孕育了丰富的文化遗产。

随着大量新石器时代岩画相继在景泰县寺滩乡、中泉镇、红水镇、正路镇和上沙沃镇被发现，这里成为中国北方岩画的代表性地区之一。这些岩画是古代游牧民族在岩石表面雕刻而成，其内容丰富、题材广泛，除了人物形象，还有动物形象，如羊、马和鹿等，主要描绘了狩猎场景和祭祀仪式。

景泰岩画被称为"刻在石头上的艺术史"，在历史、考古、艺术等多方面具有极其重要的价值和意义。景泰岩画不仅反映了古时这里的生态环境，还展示了中国早期北方游牧民族的生活状况、宗教信仰和审美观念等。

Jingtai Jiangwogou Rock Paintings

2

Administrative Division 行政区划

In September 1949, with the liberation of the Jingtai area, the People's Government of Jingtai County was established. Ever since, its affiliation has undergone several changes. From 1949 to 1955, it was under the jurisdiction of Wuwei Prefecture. From 1955 to 1959, it was administered by Dingxi Prefecture. From 1959 to 1963, it was part of Baiyin Municipality. From 1963 to 1985, it was once again under the jurisdiction of Wuwei Prefecture. Since 1985, it has been under the administration of Baiyin Municipality. The county seat was originally located in Luyang but was relocated to Yitiaoshan in 1978.

Jingtai currently has jurisdiction over 8 towns (Yitiaoshan, Luyang, Xiquan, Caowotan, Hongshui, Zhenglu, Zhongquan, Shangshawo) and 3 townships (Wufo, Sitan, Manshuitan). There are 135 administrative villages and 16 communities. Together, they form the beautiful and vibrant county of Jingtai.

1949年9月景泰地区解放后，景泰县人民政府随即诞生。此后，其行政隶属经历了多次变迁。1949年至1955年，景泰县隶属于武威地区；1955年至1959年，划归定西地区；1959年至1963年，归属白银市；1963年至1985年，再次隶属于武威地区。自1985年起，景泰县由白银市管辖至今。县城最初设在芦阳，后于1978年迁至一条山镇。

景泰县目前下辖8个镇和3个乡，分别为一条山镇、芦阳镇、喜泉镇、草窝滩镇、红水镇、正路镇、中泉镇、上沙沃镇，以及五佛乡、寺滩乡、漫水滩乡。全县共辖135个行政村和16个社区。这些行政区划共同构成了景泰县美丽多彩的版图。

3

Geographical Environment 地理环境

3.1 Geographical Location 地理位置

Located in the central part of Gansu Province, the upper reaches of the Yellow River, the transitional zone between the Loess Plateau and the Tengger Desert, and the junction of Gansu Province, Ningxia Hui Autonomous Region and Inner Mongolia Autonomous Region, Jingtai borders Jingyuan and Pingchuan on the east, Tianzhu and Gulang on the west, Baiyin, Gaolan and Yongdeng on the south, and Zhongwei and Alxa Left Banner on the north. It serves as the east gateway to the Hexi Corridor, a natural land passage stretching over a distance of around 1,000 kilometers in Gansu. The unique geographical location of Jingtai is often described by expressions like "A rooster's crow is audible in three provinces" and "Treading on three provinces with one foot".

Jingtai covers an area of 5,485 square kilometers, stretching approximately 84 kilometers from east to west and 102 kilometers from north to south. It spans from 36°43′ to 37°38′ north latitude and 103°33′ to 104°43′ east longitude. The terrain slopes from the southwest to the northeast, with elevations ranging from 1,276 to 3,321 meters above sea level.

景泰县位于甘肃省中部，黄河上游，这里是黄土高原与腾格里沙漠的交会点，也是甘肃、宁夏、内蒙古三省（区）的交界之地。景泰东接靖远县、平川区，西与天祝藏族自治县及古浪县毗邻，南和白银市、皋兰县及永登县接壤，北连宁夏中卫市和内蒙古阿拉善左旗。因其独特的地理位置，景泰县素有"鸡鸣三省"和"一脚踏三省"的美誉，是河西走廊的东端门户。

景泰县地域辽阔，总面积达到5485平方千米，东西长约84千米，南北宽约102千米。地理位置介于北纬36°43′至37°38′、东经103°33′至104°43′之间。这里地势呈现出西南高东北低的特点，海拔高度在1276米至3321米之间。

3.2 Landform 地形地貌

Jingtai is located in the upper reaches of the Yellow River and stands in the transitional zone between the Inner Mongolian Plateau and the Loess Plateau in western China. The terrain is higher in the southwest and lower in the northeast. The average altitude is 1,610 meters with the highest reaching 3,321 meters and the lowest 1,276 meters.

Around four fifths of the land lies between 1,500 meters and 2,000 meters above sea level, and three quarters of the area consists of mountains and hills, affording it a diversity of landscapes matched by few places. Mountains, canyons, forests, steppes, Gobi desert as well as wetlands can be found here. All these create a captivating picture of natural beauty.

　　景泰县是中国西部黄河上游的一颗璀璨明珠，镶嵌在内蒙古高原与黄土高原的交会地带。这里的地形呈现出西南高、东北低的自然走势，平均海拔1610米，最高处海拔3321米，最低处海拔1276米。

　　全县约百分之八十的区域海拔介于1500米至2000米之间，四分之三的土地被山地丘陵所覆盖，这种独特的地形造就了景泰县丰富多样的地貌特征。山脉、峡谷、森林、草原、戈壁沙漠和湿地等多种自然景观在这里汇聚，构成了一幅壮丽无比的自然画卷。

3.3 Climate 气候

Jingtai is dominated by an arid climate under the influence of the Tenger Desert. Spring in Jingtai is always dry and windy. The temperature changes frequently and sandstorms hit the county from time to time. In summer, the temperature is high with sufficient sunlight and rainfall increases. Sometimes sudden rainstorms would come, easily triggering flash floods, landslides and other unexpected natural disasters. It's often rainy in autumn. The temperature drops sharply with a large temperature difference between day and night. As the saying goes, it's getting colder with each autumn rain. Winter in the county is always cold and dry with occasional snowfall.

Jingtai is one of the arid counties in central Gansu Province. It enjoys an average of 2,724.3 hours of sunshine yearly. The frost - free period lasts for 198 days, with an average annual temperature of around 9.5 ℃. The average annual precipitation is approximately 195.6 mm, most of which occurs in sum-mer with the heaviest rainfall in July and August.

受腾格里沙漠的影响，景泰县气候呈现出典型的干旱特征。春季，这里气温变化频繁，气候干燥，风沙天气较多，易形成沙尘暴。夏季气温高，光照充足，降水增多。有时会有短时暴雨天气，极易引发山洪、山体滑坡等自然灾害。秋季，这里阴雨天气较多，气温下降快，昼夜温差大，正如俗语所说，"一场秋雨一场寒"。冬季气候寒冷干燥，降雪稀少。

作为甘肃省中部的干旱县之一，景泰县拥有丰富的日照资源，年平均日照时数达到2724.3小时，平均无霜期为198天，年平均气温约为9.5 ℃。年平均降水量相对较少，大约为195.6毫米，且主要集中在夏季，尤其是7月和8月，这两个月的降水最为集中。

3.4 River System 河流水系

Situated in the central part of Gansu Province, Jingtai is a key ecological preservation area along the Yellow River and one of the major grain - producing areas in the province. However, it's also an arid region with a fragile ecological environment. Water shortages are a key constraint on the socio - economic development.

The Yellow River, the second longest river in China which is known as China's "mother river" and the cradle of Chinese civilization, is the only river that flows through the region. It runs into Jingtai from Weiquan and passes through many places including Longwan, Suoqiao, Wufo and Cuiliu before entering Zhongwei in Ningxia Hui Autonomous Region, cutting through several canyons along the way. The river travels a journey of 110 kilometers within Jingtai, covering a drainage area of over 4,224 square kilometers.

The Yellow River brings Jingtai rich water resources, which are essential for local agricultural irrigation and household water supply. It not only nurtures all forms of life in the region, but also plays an irreplaceable role in promoting the local economic development and maintaining ecological balance.

景泰县地处甘肃中部，不仅是黄河重点生态保护区，也是甘肃省的主要粮食生产基地之一。然而，景泰长期面临着干旱的挑战，生态环境相对脆弱，水资源是影响全县社会经济发展的关键因素。

黄河，作为景泰县境内唯一的过境水系，从尾泉进入景泰，沿途穿越多座峡谷，流经龙湾、索桥、五佛、翠柳等地后，离开景泰县境，进入宁夏中卫市。在景泰县境内，黄河的流程长达110千米，流域面积广达4224平方千米。

黄河为景泰县带来了丰富的水资源，对于当地的农业灌溉和居民生活用水起到了不可替代的作用。它不仅是景泰县的生命之源，也是推动经济发展和维持生态平衡的关键。

An Aerial View of the Yellow River in Wufo

4

Population 人口

Located in the junction of Gansu Province, Ning-xia Hui Autonomous Region and Inner Mongolia Auton-omous Region, Jingtai is a multi‐ethnic county where people from different ethnic groups live in harmony, with frequent cultural exchanges. There are a total of 25 ethnic groups, including Han, Hui, Zang and Mongo-lian.

As of 2024, there are 71,129 households in Jingtai, with a registered population of 237,191, including an urban population of around 73,000, which accounts for 30.72% of the total. The permanent population is 196,900, with a permanent urban popula-tion of 114,900, making up 58.35%.

Over three‐quarters of the population live in the irrigated areas of the Jingtaichuan Electric Pumping Irrigation Project and the Zhongquan Electric Pumping Irrigation Project, and the flat areas along the Yellow River. The average population density is 43 people per square kilometer.

Jingtai people are known for their kindness, persistence, hospitality and sincerity. They show a deep respect for the traditions and customs and take great pride in their cultural heritage. Everyone is doing their best to make contributions to the development and prosperity of Jingtai.

Towns and townships	Number of administrative villages	Number of communities	Number of households	Registered population
Yitiaoshan	2	13	20,479	53,080
Luyang	13	1	7,015	26,797
Xiquan	17	0	6,291	23,173
Caowotan	18	0	6,670	21,601
Hongshui	15	1	5,231	19,576
Zhenglu	16	0	5,063	18,531
Zhongquan	12	0	4,383	15,970
Shangshawo	10	0	2,696	9,923
Wufo	6	0	4,437	17,587
Sitan	15	1	5,336	19,368
Manshuitan	11	0	3,438	11,585

Population of Jingtai

景泰县地处甘肃、宁夏、内蒙古三省（区）交界处，是一个多民族聚居、文化交流频繁的地区，这里汇聚了汉族、回族、藏族、蒙古族等25个民族。

截至目前，景泰县户籍总户数为71129户，户籍人口达到237191人，其中城镇人口约为7.3万人，占比30.72%。常住人口为19.69万人，其中城镇人口为11.49万人，占比高达58.35%。

全县超过四分之三的人口集中在景泰川灌区、中电灌区及黄河沿岸地势平坦地区。全县平均人口密度为每平方千米43人。

景泰人心地善良、性格坚韧、热情好客、待人真诚，对传统文化怀有深深的敬意和无比的自豪感。每一位景泰人都在为家乡的发展和繁荣贡献着自己的力量。

5

Natural Resources 自然资源

5.1 Land Resources 土地资源

Jingtai covers a total area of 5,485 square kilometers. There are 1.19 million *mu* of arable land (including 770,000 *mu* of irrigated land and 420,000 *mu* of non-irrigated land), 506,000 *mu* of woodland and 5.66 million *mu* of grassland.

Located at the golden farming belt of 37 degrees north latitude, Jingtai enjoys excellent natural conditions for the production of high-quality agricultural products, like flat terrain, fertile soil, sufficient sunshine and distinctive temperature differences between day and night. It's one of the key production bases for commodity grain in China.

景泰县总面积达5485平方千米。全县耕地面积为119万亩，包括77万亩的水浇地和42万亩的旱地，林地面积为50.6万亩，草地面积更是达到了 566 万亩。

An Aerial Drone Photo Shows Villagers Planting Rice Seedlings in Wufo

　　景泰县地处北纬 37°优质农产品黄金种植带。这里地势平坦，土壤肥沃，光照时间长，昼夜温差大，农产品质量好，是中国重要的商品粮生产基地之一。

5.2 Mineral Resources 矿产资源

　　Jingtai is under the jurisdiction of Baiyin Municipality, the only city in China named after a precious metal and known as the "Copper City". It has abundant and various mineral resources. Thirty five different minerals have been found here, with coal, gypsum and limestone standing out for their high reserves. They play a crucial role in the local socio-economic development.

　　景泰县隶属于全国唯一以金属命名的城市白银市管辖。这里以其丰富的矿产资源而闻名。已探明的矿产资源种类多达 35 种，在这些矿产资源中，煤炭、石膏、石灰石等优势明显，是推动当地社会经济发展的支柱产业。

5.2.1　Coal 煤炭

Jingtai is rich in coal, a black or brownish-black mineral that is found mainly in underground seams. The proved reserves are around 380 million tons, over 80 percent of which are distributed in the north.

It's of good quality and is widely used in various industries, such as power generation and steel production. The coal industry has made great contributions to the local economic growth.

景泰县地下蕴藏着丰富的煤炭资源，这些煤炭主要呈现黑色或深棕色。景泰县已探明的煤炭储量高达3.8亿吨，其中超过80%的煤炭资源富集于北部地区。

景泰县的煤炭以其卓越的品质而受到青睐，被广泛应用于发电和钢铁生产等多个关键行业，为当地的经济发展做出了巨大贡献。

5.2.2　Gypsum 石膏

Gypsum, a soft white mineral, is an important building material widely used in the manufacture of molds and decorative materials. Jingtai is renowned for its abundant gypsum resources. The proved reserves amount to 386 million tons, ranking second in China.

Jingtai has a long history of gypsum mining. The gypsum is of high quality and is distributed in many towns, including Caowotan, Shangshawo, Xiquan, Luyang and Zhenglu.

石膏是一种质地柔软的白色矿物，在建筑领域被广泛应用，尤其是在制造模具和装饰材料方面。景泰县的石膏资源极其丰富，储量高达3.86亿吨，位居全国第二。

景泰县石膏资源开发历史悠久，品质优良，分布广泛，主要产地有草窝滩镇、上沙沃镇、喜泉镇、芦阳镇、正路镇等。

5.2.3　Limestone 石灰石

Limestone, a whitish-colored rock, is another important building material mainly used for producing cement and calcium carbide. Jingtai boasts abundant high-quality limestone resources, which are widely distributed across the county. The proved reserves are around 800 million tons.

石灰石是一种常见的白色岩石，因其是生产水泥和电石的关键原料而成为另一种极其重要的建筑材料。景泰县各乡镇的石灰石资源不仅品质优良，而且储量丰富，全县石灰石储量高达8亿吨。

5.3 Wind Power 风能资源

Located in the transitional zone between the monsoon and non‑monsoon regions, Jingtai is one of the counties with the most abundant wind resources in Gansu Province. The locals often joke that wind only comes once a year in Jingtai, but it lasts from spring to winter. Though a bit exaggerated, it indicates that the region is particularly rich in wind power, one of the cleanest sources of energy and an alternative to fossil fuels.

The dominant wind direction in Jingtai is NW. The average annual wind speed is 2.9 meters per second, with the maximum wind speed reaching 21.7 meters per second. The theoretical reserve of wind energy is around 2,000 MW. Thus, there's a great potential for the development and utilization of wind power in the county. Over the past decade, Jingtai has seen rapid growth in wind power, with many wind power plants installed and put into operation. The cumulative installed capacity of wind power has reached 1.14 million kilowatts.

景泰县地处季风区与非季风区的过渡地带，这一独特的地理位置赋予了它丰富的风能资源，使其成为甘肃省风能资源最丰富的县区之一。当地人常戏言"一年一场风，从春刮到冬"。虽然这种说法略显夸张，但也反映了景泰县风能资源的丰富程度。

景泰县全年主要风向为西北风，年平均风速为每秒2.9米，最大风速每秒21.7米。其风能理论储量约2000兆瓦，这一巨大的储量预示着景泰县在风能资源开发利用方面的极大潜力。近十年，景泰风电发展迅速，许多风电场已建成并投入使用。全县风电总装机容量达114万千瓦。

Datang Jingtai Wind Farm

5.4 Solar Energy 太阳能资源

Jingtai, one of the regions with particularly abundant solar resources in China, has less rainfall, longer sunshine hours, and stronger sunlight radiation. It enjoys around 2,725 hours of sunshine annually and the percentage of sunshine is 60%. The annual solar radiation reaches 147.8 kcal per square centimeters.

As a green and renewable energy, solar energy has been highly valued by the local government. In recent years, Jingtai has quickened its steps toward the development of solar energy. Many photovoltaic power generation stations have been set and more are under construction. The cumulative installed capacity of photovoltaics has reached 729,000 kilowatts. In years to come, the photovoltaic industry in Jingtai will see further growth. It will drive the regional economic growth and benefit the local residents.

An Aerial Photo Shows a Photovoltaic Power Plant in Jingtai

　　景泰县年均日照时数为2725小时，日照百分率为60%，太阳年平均辐射量为147.8千卡/平方厘米。这里降雨稀少、日照时间长、光照强度大，是全国太阳能资源的富集区之一。

　　太阳能作为一种清洁、可再生能源，得到了当地政府的高度重视和积极推动。景泰县的光伏产业正在迅速崛起，众多光伏发电厂已相继建成。全县光伏总装机容量达72.9万千瓦。未来，景泰光伏产业将得到进一步发展，为当地经济的增长和百姓的福祉提供更强有力的支持。

6

Transportation 交通运输

Located in the junction of Gansu Province, Ningxia Hui Autonomous Region and Inner Mongolia Autonomous Region, Jingtai, a key node on the ancient Silk Road, is the east gateway to the Hexi Corridor, also known as the Gansu Corridor. It's been a key transportation hub from ancient times to the present. It's 180 kilometers south of Lanzhou, the capital of Gansu Province, 300 kilometers north of Yinchuan, the capital of Ningxia Hui Autonomous Region, 90 kilometers southeast of Baiyin and 220 kilometers northwest of Wuwei.

Today, Jingtai boasts a highly convenient transportation system, providing great convenience for the locals' traveling and accelerating the development of the local economy. 2 railways (Baotou - Lanzhou Railway and Gantang - Wuwei Railway), 2 expressways (Yingpanshui - Shuangta Expressway and Jingtai - Zhongchuan Airport Expressway), 2 national highways (G338 and G247) and 5 provincial highways (S101, S103,

S217, S308 and S315) run across the county. Besides, a large number of county-level highways and rural roads reach all corners of the county, connecting smaller towns and villages. All of them form a transportation network that extends in all directions.

　　景泰县位于甘肃、宁夏、内蒙古三省（区）交界处，是丝绸之路上的重要节点，河西走廊的东端门户。景泰南距甘肃省会兰州180千米，北距宁夏首府银川300千米，东南距白银90千米，西北距武威220千米，自古以来交通位置就十分重要。

　　如今，景泰县交通网络更是纵横交错，极大地便利了人们的出行，并为当地经济的蓬勃发展提供了强劲动力。截至目前，已有2条铁路（包兰铁路、干武铁路）、2条高速公路（营双高速、景中高速）、2条国道（G338、G247）、5条省道（S101、S103、S217、S308、S315）穿过县域。此外，景泰县还有许多县道和乡村公路，纵横交织，串联起了景泰县的各个角落。这些道路共同构建起景泰四通八达的交通网络。

The Jingtai South Toll Station on the Jingtai-Zhongchuan Airport Expressway

7

Education and Health Care 教育医疗

7.1 Education 教育事业

There are 110 schools（29 kindergartens，66 elementary schools，12 middle schools，2 high schools and 1 vocational school），3,510 teachers（403 in kindergartens，1,625 in elementary schools，858 in middle schools，490 in high schools and 134 in the vocational school）and 34,051 students（5,665 in kindergartens，15,131 in primary schools，7,475 in middle schools，4,903 in high schools and 877 in the vocational school）in Jingtai.

Education development is set as a top priority in Jingtai. In recent years，the local authorities have taken various measures to improve education with a focus on developing high-quality and well-balanced compulsory education. Significant efforts have been made to upgrade the facilities in rural schools and build a team of competent rural teachers，who are dedicated to helping rural children move ahead. Furthermore, the local government has devoted great energy to strengthening the professional ethics of teachers, optimizing the system of teacher management and training, improving teachers' abilities and enhancing students' well-rounded development.

In 2024, Jingtai achieved new highs in both the average score of the High School Entrance Examination(HSEE)and the undergraduate admission rate. Jingtai's HSEE average score has ranked first in Baiyin for seven consecutive years. Moreover, many students from Jingtai Vocational School have won awards in the Vocational Students Skills Competition of Gansu Province.

景泰县现有各级各类学校110所，其中幼儿园29所、小学66所、初中12所、高中2所、职业中专1所。全县共有教师3510名，其中幼儿园教师403名、小学教师1625名、初中教师858名、高中教师490名、职业中专教师134名。在校学生总数为34051名，其中幼儿园学生5665名、小学生15131名、初中生7475名、高中生4903名、职业中专学生877名。

景泰县坚持教育优先发展，近年来不断推动义务教育优质均衡发展，大力改善乡村学校办学条件，加强乡村教师队伍建设，关注留守儿童发展。同时，景泰县不断加强师德师风建设，优化教师管理、培训体系，提升教师业务能力，大力发展素质教育。

2024年景泰县中高考成绩再创历史新高，中考成绩连续七年蝉联全市第一。同时，景泰职业中专多名学生在甘肃省职业院校技能大赛中获奖。

7.1.1　Jingtai No.1 High School 景泰县第一中学

Jingtai No.1 High School is a municipal-level demonstrative high school in Baiyin, with a history that can be traced back to 1945. After 79-year development, the school has formed valuable traditions and distinguished features as reflected by its motto "Sound in Morality and Broad in Learning".

The campus covers a total area of 262 *mu*, with 2,640 students and 245 faculty members. The library houses more than 120,000 books and magazines. A wide range of rich and colorful activities are organized and conducted to cater to the diverse needs of the students and promote their all-round development.

In recent years, Jingtai No.1 High School, with brilliant teachers and advanced teaching facilities, has received numerous accolades, such as "National Youth Campus Football Characteristic School", "Advanced Unit for Air Force Recruitment", "Advanced Unit of Baiyin Education System", and "Model School of Moral Education".

Since its founding, the school has seen a large number of graduates admitted to top-tier universities in China, including Tsinghua University, Peking University and Zhejiang University, and they are making remarkable achievements and contributions all around the world.

Jingtai No.1 High School

　　景泰县第一中学是一所历史悠久的学校。自1945年成立以来，学校秉承"厚德博学"的校训，已经走过了79年的光辉历程，现已发展成为白银市一所具有优良传统和鲜明特色的市级示范化高中。

　　学校占地面积广阔，达到262亩。目前，学校共有2640名学生和245名教职员工。学校图书馆藏书丰富，拥有12万余册图书。学校注重学生的全面发展，积极组织和开展丰富多彩的校园活动，满足学生的多元化需求，为学生提供全方位的成长支持。

　　景泰县第一中学师资力量雄厚，教学设施先进，教学成果显著。近年来，学校多次获得表彰和奖励，如"全国青少年校园足球特色学校""空军招飞工作先进单位""白银市教育系统先进集体""德育示范学校"等荣誉称号。

　　自建校以来，大批毕业生考入清华大学、北京大学、浙江大学等国内顶尖大学，并在各自的领域取得了令人瞩目的成就。

7.1.2　Jingtai No.2 High School 景泰县第二中学

Jingtai No.2 High School, founded in 1979, is a municipal-level demonstrative high school in Baiyin. It covers an area of 108 *mu*, with more than 240 faculty members and over 2,500 students. The library houses over 106,000 books and magazines.

Guided by the school philosophy of "Everything for the development of students, teachers and the school", it's characterized by its focus on humanistic education and independent development. The school emphasizes students' self-management, advocates humanistic education and attaches great importance to moral practice. In recent years, it has received many accolades, including "National Youth Campus Basketball Characteristic School", "Provincial Civilized Campus" and "Advanced Unit of Baiyin Education System".

With advanced teaching facilities and a team of outstanding teachers, the garden-like school is well known for its strict approach in pursuing studies. It has been constantly making steps and creating new brilliance. Over the nearly 46 years since it was established, many graduates have been accepted into

China's first-tier universities, such as Tsinghua University, Peking University and Fudan University, and are making significant contributions in various fields.

　　景泰县第二中学始建于1979年，是白银市市级示范性高中。学校占地面积108亩，现有教职工240多人，学生2500余名，图书馆藏书超过10.6万册。

　　学校始终秉持"一切为了学生的发展，一切为了教师的发展，一切为了学校的发展"的办学理念，以人文教育和自主发展为特色。学校尊重学生的自我管理，倡导人文教育，高度重视品德培养。近年来，学校多次获得表彰和奖励，包括"全国青少年篮球特色学校""省级文明校园""白银市教育系统先进集体"等荣誉称号。

　　景泰县第二中学教学设施先进，师资力量雄厚，校园优美，治学严谨。学校砥砺前行，不断追求卓越，创造新的辉煌。自建校以来，众多毕业生被清华大学、北京大学、复旦大学等国内顶尖高校录取，并在各行各业做出了非凡的贡献。

Jingtai No.2 High School

7.1.3 Jingtai Vocational School 景泰县职业中等专业学校

Jingtai Vocational School, founded in 1984, is a national key vocational school. It covers an area of 120 *mu*, with 134 teachers and more than 800 students.

The school has devoted great energy to cultivating inquiring, knowledgeable, confident, caring and application-oriented talents, who are willing to take responsibilities and conscious of showing gratitude. The teachers work tirelessly to impart the students essential skills and values, preparing them for future success after graduation.

In recent years, the graduates have been greatly welcomed by employers and the employment rate has remained consistently high. Many have achieved remarkable accomplishments in their respective fields.

Jingtai Vocational School

景泰县职业中等专业学校自1984年创建以来，已经发展成为一所国家级重点职业学校。学校占地面积达到120亩，现有教师134人，学生800余名。

景泰职中着力于培养善于探究、知识丰富、有自信、有爱心、有担当、懂感恩的应用型人才。学校高度重视学生专业技能的学习，以帮助他们在当今快速发展的社会中取得成功。

近年来，职中毕业生在人才市场上备受青睐，就业率始终保持在较高水平。许多优秀毕业生已经成为各自领域中的佼佼者。

7.2 Health Care 医疗

There are 230 medical institutions, including 3 public hospitals (The People's Hospital of Jingtai, The Hospital of Traditional Chinese Medicine of Jingtai, The Maternity and Child-care Hospital of Jingtai), 2 professional public health institutions, 1 private hospital and 11 township-level medical institutions in Jingtai.

Consistently guided by the needs of patients, the medical workers tirelessly devote themselves to providing the best services with their solid faith, professional ethics, unreserved contribution, and rigorous academic attitude.

景泰县共有各级各类医疗卫生机构230家，其中公立医疗机构3家（景泰县人民医院、景泰县中医医院、景泰县妇幼保健院）、专业公共卫生机构2家、民营医院1家、乡镇卫生院11家。

全县卫健系统医务人员始终以患者需求为导向，以坚定的理想信念、崇高的职业道德、无私的奉献精神、严谨的学术态度，为患者提供最优质的服务。

7.2.1　The People's Hospital of Jingtai 景泰县人民医院

Located at No. 638, Yongtai Road, Yitiaoshan, the People's Hospital of Jingtai was founded in 1956. It covers a total area of 30,000 square meters, with a construction area of 22,000 square meters. It's a comprehensive Second-level Grade-A hospital integrating medical treatment, first aid, disease prevention, scientific research and teaching. There are 19 clinical departments, 9 medical and technical departments, 499 authorized beds, and 465 employees.

Over the years, the People's Hospital of Jingtai has been adhering to the principle of prioritizing patients' needs. It is committed to cultivating medical talents, accelerating the construction of basic facilities, and continuously improving its medical level. In recognition of its achievements, the hospital was rated as a "Second-level Grade A Hospital" by the Ministry of Health in 1996, a "Baby-friendly Hospital" by the World Health Organization, the International Children's Fund and the Ministry of Health in 1997, an "Advanced Civilized Unit" by Baiyin Municipal People's Government in 2014, and a "Provincial Civilized Unit" by the Gansu Provincial Committee of the Party and Provincial Government in 2018.

Today, with its dedicated medical workers and advanced medical equipment, the People's Hospital of Jingtai plays a significant role in safeguarding the health and well-being of Jingtai people.

The People's Hospital of Jingtai

景泰县人民医院位于一条山镇永泰路638号，医院占地面积达到3万平方米，建筑面积为2.2万平方米。自1956年建院以来，县人民医院已发展成为一所集医疗、急救、疾病预防、科研、教学为一体的综合性二级甲等医院。医院设有临床科室19个，医技科室9个，床位499张，员工465人。

景泰县人民医院多年来始终坚持以病人为中心，以人才培养为重点，加速基础建设，不断提高医疗水平。1996年医院被卫生部评为二级甲等医院，1997年被世界卫生组织、国际儿童基金会和卫生部评为"爱婴医院"，2014年被白银市政府评为"先进文明单位"，2018年被甘肃省委省政府评为"省级文明单位"。

如今，景泰县人民医院不仅汇集了一大批优秀的医务人员，还配备了先进的医疗设备，这使其在保障全县人民生命健康方面发挥着至关重要的作用。

7.2.2　The Hospital of Traditional Chinese Medicine （TCM） of Jingtai 景泰县中医医院

Located at No. 335, Nanshan Road, Yitiaoshan, the Hospital of Traditional Chinese Medicine (TCM) of Jingtai was established in 1984. It covers an area of 127.5 *mu* with a construction area of 42,000 square meters. It's a comprehensive Second - level Grade - A hospital of traditional Chinese medicine integrating medical treatment, teaching, scientific research, first aid, disease prevention, rehabilitation and physical examination. There are 17 clinical departments, 11 medical and technical departments, 499 authorized beds, and 375 employees.

The Hospital of Traditional Chinese Medicine （TCM） of Jingtai consistently adheres to the spirit of innovation and a patient - centered service philosophy. It places equal emphasis on both traditional Chinese medicine （TCM） and Western medicine with special support for TCM. In recognition of its excellence, the hospital was rated as a "Second - level Grade - A Hospital of TCM" by the Health and Family Planning Commission of Gansu Province in September 2002. It was also honored as a "Provincial Advanced Collective of

Traditional Chinese Medicine" by the Health Commission of Gansu Province in May 2020 and a "Provincial March 8th Red - Banner Collective" by the Department of Human Resources and Social Security of Gansu Province and the Gansu Provincial Women's Federation in December 2022.

　　景泰县中医医院始建于1984年，位于一条山镇南山路335号，是一所集医疗、教学、科研、急救、疾病预防、康复、健康体检于一体的综合性二级甲等中医医院。医院占地面积为127.5亩，总建筑面积达到4.2万平方米。医院现有17个临床科室，11个医技科室，床位499张，职工375人。

　　景泰县中医医院始终坚持创新精神和以病人为中心的服务理念，强调中西医并重，大力发展中医药事业。2002年9月，医院被甘肃省卫生和计划生育委员会评定为二级甲等中医医院，2020年5月被甘肃省卫生健康委员会授予"全省中医药工作先进集体"称号，2022年12月被甘肃省人力资源和社会保障厅、甘肃省妇女联合会授予"甘肃省三八红旗集体"称号。

The Hospital of Traditional Chinese Medicine of Jingtai

8

Folk Culture 民俗文化

Located in central Gansu Province and the upper reaches of the Yellow River, Jingtai, a county under the administration of Baiyin Municipality, has a long history and profound cultural heritage, making it one of the most culturally rich counties in Gansu Province. It's blessed with abundant historical and cultural resources, such as Jingtai Shehuo, Rolling Lantern Dance, Molten Iron Fireworks, Jingtai Ditty, Bark - brush Painting, Paper - cutting, Embroidery, etc. These cultural treasures not only reflect the wisdom and creativity of Jingtai people but also serve as important windows into the rich history and vibrant culture of the region.

景泰县位于甘肃省中部、黄河上游，隶属于白银市。这片土地历史悠久，文化底蕴深厚，孕育了丰富多彩的历史文化遗产，如景泰社火、滚灯、打铁花、景泰小曲、树皮笔画、剪纸、刺绣等。这些文化瑰宝不仅反映了景泰人民的智慧和创造力，也是了解当地历史和文化的重要窗口。

8.1 Jingtai Shehuo 景泰社火

Jingtai Shehuo is a time - honored custom deeply rooted in the local culture. It originated from ancient sacrificial activities thousands of years ago. Over the centuries, it has evolved into a grand celebration, incorporating diverse elements, such as dance, music, drama, etc. "She" originally means the God of Earth and "Huo" refers to the God of Fire. In ancient times, people regarded the earth, which was for farming, and the fire, which was for cooking and warming, as two fundamental basis of living.

Emerging in feudal times, Jingtai Shehuo acted as a vital medium through which people expressed their inner feelings and got spiritual comfort and support. It has high artistic value for the exquisite props, distinctive facial makeups, beautiful lyrics, and novel and mysterious performances. It's also of great significance for the study of local history and culture.

Jingtai Shehuo is composed of multiple performances, such as dragon dance, lion dance, land boat dance, stilt walking, yangge dance, drum playing, etc. Dressed in ancient costumes and adorned with distinctive facial makeups, performers use props to ward off evil spirits, honor deities and pray for bountiful harvests, fortune and prosperity. Among these performances, dragon dances stand out as a highlight. In Chinese traditional culture, the dragon is a symbol of wisdom, strength, good fortune and wealth. As the dragon dances its way, accompanied by the rhythmic beating of drums, it symbolizes the coming of a good year.

Today, Jingtai Shehuo, usually taking place around the Lantern Festival, a major Chinese festival celebrated on the fifteenth day of the first lunar month, is a celebration that involves a large number of performers. The majority of villagers will participate either in the performance or the preparation work. It brings people together, regardless of age or background, to share the spirit and joy of the occasion. It not only preserves the ancient traditions but also serves as a platform for people to showcase their talents, skills and their passion for life.

Performers Play Drums during a Shehuo Show in Jingtai

　　景泰社火起源于几千年前的祭祀活动，历史悠久，源远流长。如今，景泰社火已演变成融合了音乐、舞蹈、戏剧等多种元素的盛大庆祝活动。最初，"社"和"火"分别象征着土地神和火神，反映了古人对耕作土地和烹饪取暖之火的崇敬，这两者也被视为生活的基石。

　　景泰社火是封建时代人民情感表达、心灵慰藉和精神寄托的重要艺术形式，其精美的道具、独特的脸谱、生动的唱词和新奇的表演，都彰显了其高超的艺术价值，对于研究当地的人文历史具有不可估量的意义。

　　景泰社火的表现形式丰富多样，涵盖了舞龙、舞狮、划旱船、踩高跷、扭秧歌、击鼓等多种民俗活动。表演者通常着古装，画脸谱，手持"法器"来驱邪、敬神、祈求五谷丰登以及财运亨通。舞龙是社火的重头戏。龙的形象在中国传统文化中是智慧、力量、好运和财富的象征。伴随着激昂的鼓声，祥龙上下翻飞，展现出恢宏的气势，象征着美好一年的到来。

如今，景泰社火已成为每年元宵节前后不可或缺的群众性节庆活动，村里的大多数人都会参与到社火的准备工作或表演中。届时人们欢聚一堂，沉浸在这个节日的欢乐气氛中。景泰社火不仅延续了古老的传统，还成为人们展示自己才华的舞台，更是他们对生活热爱之情的自然流露。

8.2 Rolling Lantern Dance 滚灯

The Rolling Lantern Dance, included in the fourth batch of Gansu provincial intangible cultural heritage list in 2017, is a well-known folk performance that originated in Jingtai and has gained widespread popularity both in the region and beyond.

According to literature, beacon towers were built along the Great Wall in ancient times. The troops stationed on the wall used smoke during the day and fire at night to send warning signals. Over time, the light that once signaled alarms gradually evolved into the Rolling Lantern Dance.

With a history of over 300 years, it has become an indispensable art performance at the Lantern Festival and other major celebrations in Jingtai. When the performance begins, the performers vigorously roll the lanterns to the rhythmic beats of gongs and drums. The lanterns sometimes appear like a sea of blooming flowers and sometimes a flying dragon, fully and vividly demonstrating the unique charm of the centuries-old art form. It's truly a feast for the eyes.

Years ago, the Rolling Lantern Dance was in danger of dying out because there were fewer people who could perform it and most of them were in their sixties. The Cultural Center of Jingtai took effective measures to preserve this precious folk art. Through the joint efforts of cultural workers and folk artists, it has constantly made innovations and become more artistically charming. Furthermore, increasing participation from local residents has helped the Rolling Lantern Dance continue to thrive and be passed down through generations.

　　滚灯是景泰县著名的民俗表演艺术，于2017年被列入甘肃省非物质文化遗产名录，深受人们喜爱。据史料记载，古代长城沿线设烽火台，昼夜分别用烟和光传递军情，这一传统随着时间的推移逐渐演变成今天我们所看到的滚灯表演，其历史已有300多年。如今，滚灯已成为景泰县元宵节及其他重大节日中不可或缺的艺术形式。表演开始后，舞动的滚灯时而如同绚烂的花海，时而宛如腾空的巨龙，令人目不暇接，美不胜收。

　　几年前，能够表演滚灯的民间艺人寥寥无几，且大多已年逾花甲。为了保护这一珍贵的非物质文化遗产，景泰县文化馆采取了积极的措施。经过多年的不懈努力，滚灯不断创新，更具艺术感染力。同时，越来越多的群众加入滚灯表演的行列中，使得这一文化遗产得以在舞台上继续传承与活跃。

Rolling Lantern Dance

8.3 Molten Iron Fireworks 打铁花

The Molten Iron Fireworks, also known as Datiehua, are a traditional form of fireworks with great popularity in Jingtai. It was included in the fourth batch of Gansu provincial intangible cultural heritage list in 2017.

With a history of more than 400 years, its origin can be traced back to the Ming Dynasty (1368–1644). Legend has it that Zhang Tiedan, a local blacksmith, first performed it with his special skills to celebrate the Spring Festival. People from Luyang and neighboring villages, men and women, young and old, gathered at the square and took great delight in watching the breathtaking show. It quickly gained popularity and became a beloved tradition.

Today, the Molten Iron Fireworks are usually staged at the Lantern Festival, celebrated on January 15th on Chinese lunar calendar, in Jingtai. The festival is considered incomplete without it. At the start of the show, scrap iron is heated in a furnace until it melts. As performers throw the molten iron into the sky with big ladles, dazzling sparks light up the sky and rain down like fireworks, creating a grand and fabulous spectacle. It's considered as one of the most special and eye-catching folk arts in Jingtai.

Molten Iron Fireworks

打铁花是景泰地区一种独特的传统烟花表演艺术，于2017年被列入甘肃省非物质文化遗产名录。

打铁花历史悠久，最早可追溯至明代，距今已有400多年的传承。在明朝时期，每逢春节，当地铁匠张铁蛋便会以其精湛的技艺表演打铁花，为节日增添浓厚的喜庆气氛。届时，芦阳及其周边地区的居民，无论男女老少，都会从四面八方汇聚于广场，共同见证这一视觉盛宴。

如今，打铁花已成为景泰每年农历正月十五不可或缺的节日盛事。表演伊始，表演者将铁片熔于火炉中。当熔化的铁水被抛向天空时，铁水在空中瞬间绽放，犹如天女散花般倾泻而下，构成了一幅美轮美奂、壮观无比的画面，这也使得打铁花成为景泰县最独特、最赏心悦目的民间艺术之一。

8.4 Jingtai Ditty 景泰小曲

Originating in Sitan, Jingtai ditty is a popular and down-to-earth traditional folk art with specific characteristics typical of the region. With a history spanning over 1,000 years, its origin can date back to the Tang Dynasty (618–907). It was included in the fifth batch of Gansu provincial intangible cultural heritage list in 2024.

Jingtai ditty is typically performed in the local dialect with instrumental accompaniments. It gains great popularity among the locals for the light-hearted and easy-to-sing melodies, and story-telling lyrics. The ditties mainly tell of traditional virtues, heroic deeds, young love, the hard work of farming life, etc.

As an important medium for expressing personal feelings and a popular rural entertainment, it's a vivid oral record of local social life, and is highly valued for its historic, literary and social significance. It plays a crucial role in carrying forward traditional culture, enriching people's cultural lives and building up cultural confidence.

景泰小曲是流行于景泰地区的一种传统民间艺术，具有浓郁的地方特色，其历史悠久，最早可追溯至唐朝。2024年景泰小曲被列入第五批甘肃省非物质文化遗产名录。

景泰小曲以地方语言演唱，搭配传统乐器伴奏，旋律简单易唱，歌词生动活泼，或弘扬传统美德，或歌颂英雄壮举，或描绘浪漫爱情故事，或表达田间劳作的辛勤劳苦，深受当地群众喜爱。

景泰小曲不仅能抒发群众的内心情感，放松身心，还能反映当地社会生活的真实面貌，具有较高的历史、文学和社会价值，在弘扬中国传统文化、丰富百姓文化生活、树立文化自信等方面发挥着重要的作用。

Jingtai Ditty

8.5 Bark-brush Painting 树皮笔画

Bark - brush painting is a unique local folk art originating in Fangcao Village, Luyang. The painting is done on Xuan paper with an ink - dipped brush made of bark. No one knows exactly when this art form was first invented. However, legend has it that the ancestor of the Li family in Fangcao Village was already one of the most influencial painters in the region in the Ming Dynasty (1368–1644). In 2017, it was included in the fourth batch of Gansu provincial intangible cultural heritage list. Li Shangxiu, Li Shangren and Li Shangyi are the representative inheritors.

The paintings are mainly themed with figures, flowers and landscapes. The artists skillfully apply the traditional techniques to the paintings. With a natural, simple and distinctive style, each piece is vivid and captivating, showing the artists' mastery and creativity.

Bark-brush Painting

Bark-brush painting is regarded as a treasure of Chinese art and culture. It reflects the profound traditional culture and the national spirit, and reveals people's yearning for a better life and a brighter future.

树皮笔画起源于景泰县芦阳镇芳草村，是用树皮做的画笔蘸墨在宣纸上作画的民间艺术。树皮笔画具体形成年代不详，据传芳草李氏先祖明代即是地方极具影响的民间绘画艺人。2017年树皮笔画被列入第四批甘肃省非物质文化遗产名录，代表性传承人有李尚秀、李尚仁、李尚义等。

树皮笔画以人物、花卉、风景为主要题材，将传统的水墨画技巧结合于绘画中，风格自然朴实，作品栩栩如生，展现出了画者高超的技艺。

树皮笔画被誉为中国艺术和文化宝库中的一朵奇葩，它蕴含着深厚的传统文化和民族精神，反映了人民群众对美好生活的向往和追求。

8.6 Jingtai Paper-cutting 景泰剪纸

Paper-cutting is one of the oldest folk arts in China. Its origin can be traced back to the Western Han Dynasty (202 BC–8 AD) after the invention of paper, with the earliest paper-cuts in existence dating back to the Northern Dynasties (386–581). During the Ming and Qing dynasties (1368–1911), paper-cutting reached its peak of craftsmanship and popularity. In 2009, it was inscribed on UNESCO's Representative List of the Intangible Cultural Heritage of Humanity.

Jingtai people have been obsessed with paper-cutting. They skillfully use scissors to cut papers into different patterns, such as animals, flowers, figures and Chinese characters. It requires great patience and concentration because even a small mistake may ruin the whole piece.

Jingtai paper-cuts are usually seen on festive occasions, such as the Lunar New Year and weddings. On Lunar New Year's Eve, paper cuts of Chinese character "福" or "blessings" in English are attached upside down to front doors as it is believed when "福" is put upside down, happiness arrives. Paper-cuts of various patterns can also be found on windows during the festival, symbolizing health and prosperity. At wedding ceremonies, paper cuts of Chinese character "囍" or "Double Happiness" in English are put up on walls, windows, doors and even furniture as symbols of wishes for a perfect marriage and life-long love.

剪纸是中国最古老的民间艺术之一，其历史可追溯至西汉时期，并在明清时期达到鼎盛。现存最早的剪纸作品出自北朝时期。这一艺术形式在2009年被联合国教科文组织列入"人类非物质文化遗产代表作名录"。

A Paper-cut of "Fu"

在景泰，剪纸广受欢迎，人们用剪刀在纸上剪出动物、花草、人物、汉字等丰富多样的图案。这一过程需要极大的耐心和专注，因为一个小错误就可能会毁掉整个作品。

景泰剪纸在春节、婚礼等喜庆场合中扮演着重要角色。春节期间，人们将剪纸"福"字倒贴在门上，寓意着福气的到来。同时，人们会在窗户上贴上象征健康和兴旺的窗花来增添节日的喜庆气氛。在婚礼上，剪纸"囍"字被用来装饰墙面、窗户、门甚至家具，以此来祝福新人婚姻美满、百年好合。

8.7 Jingtai Embroidery 景泰刺绣

Embroidery is a traditional Chinese handicraft with a long history. The earliest existing embroidery are two pieces of Warring States Period embroidery unearthed from Chu tomb in Changsha, Hunan Province.

Jingtai enjoys a thousand-year tradition of embroidery. The locals stitch colored patterns, such as landscapes, figures, flowers and animals, onto cloth using threads of various colors to create exquisite embroidery works, which carry the rich history and culture of Jingtai. In ancient times, girls in the region had to learn the embroidery skills at their early age, which would give them an advantage when they were going to get married.

Jingtai embroidery, included in the fifth batch of Gansu provincial intangible cultural heritage list in 2024, can be found on quilt covers, pillowcases and garments as decorations. Nowadays, with the elegant colors, and vivid and delicate patterns, it has become increasingly popular. It's not only a form of art to showcase beauty but also a medium to express personal feelings.

Jingtai Embroidery

刺绣是历史悠久的中国传统民间艺术。现存最早的刺绣作品是出土于湖南长沙楚墓中的两件战国时期的刺绣。

景泰有上千年的刺绣传统。人们用针线在织物上绣出风景、人物、花卉、动物等丰富多样的装饰图案。这些刺绣作品承载着景泰深厚的历史和文化。在古代，景泰地区的女孩们从小就开始学习刺绣技巧，这也是她们在婚嫁时展示才华的重要方式。

2024年，景泰刺绣被列入省级非物质文化遗产名录。它被广泛用于装饰被套、枕套、服装、鞋子等日常生活用品。景泰刺绣色彩典雅、图案精美，不仅是一种展示美的艺术形式，也是一种人们表达情感的方式。

9

Tourist Attractions 旅游景点

Located in the central part of Gansu Province, the upper reaches of the Yellow River and the transitional zone between the Loess Plateau and the Tengger Desert, Jingtai is home to a wealth of historical relics and diverse natural landscapes like majestic mountains, spectacular canyons, lush forests, boundless Gobi desert, beautiful wetlands, vast grasslands, the surging Yellow River and the winding Great Wall, making it a popular tourist destination in western China.

There are a great many famous tourist attractions, such as the Yellow River Stone Forest Scenic Area, the National Forest Park of Mount Shoulu, Yongtai Ancient Fort, Wufo Temple, the Ruins of Suoqiao Ancient Ferry, Dadunhuang Film Studio, the National Saltmarsh Wetland Park of Baidunzi, Mount Wutong, Shuigou Wetland Park, the Memorial Park of the Formation of the West Route Army in Jingtai, Xindunwan Grassland, Xifan Caves, Honggou Danxia Landform, Shuanglong Temple, Dashuizha Village and Huada Ski Resort, drawing a large number of tourists from home and abroad every year. Whether you are exploring the incredible natural scenery or enjoying yourself in the rich history and culture, Jingtai promises an unforgettable travel experience.

景泰县地处甘肃省中部、黄河上游、黄土高原与腾格里沙漠的过渡地带，是中国西部著名的旅游胜地。这里历史遗迹众多，自然风景多样，巍峨的高山、壮丽的峡谷、茂密的森林、无垠的戈壁沙漠、秀美的湿地、辽阔的草原，以及奔腾的黄河和蜿蜒的长城等景观交相辉映。

景泰境内拥有黄河石林风景区、寿鹿山国家森林公园、永泰古城、五佛寺、索桥古渡遗址、大敦煌影视城、白墩子盐沼国家湿地公园、梧桐山、水沟湿地公园、西路军景泰组成纪念园、新墩湾草原、西番窑、红沟丹霞、双龙寺、大水磴村、华达滑雪场等众多旅游景点。这些景点每年吸引着大量国内外游客前来参观游览。无论你是来探寻壮丽的自然风光，还是来了解当地丰富的历史文化，景泰都能让你的旅行留下难忘的记忆。

9.1 Yellow River Stone Forest Scenic Area
黄河石林风景区

Spanning an impressive area of approximately 10 square kilometers and known as "a natural wonder of China", the Yellow River Stone Forest Scenic Area sits at Longwan (Dragon Bay), a picturesque village in southeastern Jingtai which was named one of the top ten most beautiful villages in China in 2013 and was included in the list of China's beautiful leisure villages of 2016. It's 70 km to Baiyin and 140 km to Lanzhou, the capital city of Gansu Province, in the south, 70 km to the county seat of Jingtai in the northwest and 65 km to Jingyuan in the east.

The Yellow River Stone Forest was discovered by a fieldwork team of the

Ministry of Nuclear Industry in 1990. However, owing to its remote location and inconvenient transportation, it remained beyond tourists' reach until the road to the scenic area was completed. The stone forest, a "geological museum" sculpted by nature, was shaped about 4 million years ago as a result of collective forces of crustal movement, weathering, rain erosion as well as gravity collapse. It serves as an important record of the region's geological evolution and ancient environmental changes. There are numerous hundred-meter high stone pillars that are both magnificent in shape and vivid in form, resembling a dense forest of stones. Some of these pillars reach heights of up to 200 meters. Moreover, the Yellow River winds its way at the foot of the forest, forming a giant "S" shape. This unique combination of towering pillars and the meandering river creates a spectacular and breathtaking view that is rarely seen in other places.

The Yellow River Stone Forest Scenic Area is a national geological park, a provincial reserve of geological heritage and a national 4A tourist attraction, the second-highest in China's tourist attraction rating system. It integrates rare geological structures, stunning natural views, a long history and rich culture heritage. With its tranquil environment, fresh air and amazing scenery, the scenic area is like a land of fantasy. It was included in the *New York Times*' list of 52 Places to Go in 2018 and was listed as one of the Top 50 Scenic Spots Along the Yellow River in 2019.

The scenic area is also a popular place for filmmakers. The movies and television works shot here, such as *The Myth*, *Mulan*, *Pretty Big Feet*, *The Last Winter Day*, *World Granary*, *Star Chaser* and *Dad, Where Are We Going?*, have further enhanced its reputation.

被誉为"中华自然奇观"的黄河石林风景区坐落于景泰县东南部的龙湾村。龙湾村以其卓越的自然美景在2013年荣获"全国十大最美乡村"的美誉，并于2016年入选"中国美丽休闲乡村"名单。风景区占地约10平方千米，地理位置优越，南距白银70千米、兰州140千米，西北距景泰县城70千米，东距靖远65千米。

黄河石林于1990年被核工业部地质队发现。然而，由于当时交通不便，直到通往景区的道路建成，这一壮丽的自然风光才得以展现在世人面前。黄河石林的形成可追溯至400万年前，是地壳运动、风化、雨蚀、重力坍塌等地质作用共同塑造的自然杰作，清晰地记录了该地区的地质演变和环境变化过程。景区内石柱林立，高度多在百米以上，最高200多米，其造型雄伟，形象生动，宛若一片石头森林。此外，黄河在石林脚下蜿蜒而行，形成了一个巨大的S形弯。高耸的石柱和蜿蜒的黄河造就了一幅壮观绝伦、令人叹为观止的风景。

黄河石林风景区是一座集地质构造、自然景观、历史和文化于一体的国家级地质公园，也是甘肃省地质遗迹自然保护区和国家4A级景区。景区环境幽静，空气清新，风景别具神韵，让人仿佛置身于梦幻之境。2018年，《纽约时报》将黄河石林评为"全球必去的52个目的地"之一，2019年又被评为"中国黄河50景"之一。

黄河石林同时也是中国著名的影视拍摄胜地，众多影视剧如《神话》《花木兰》《美丽的大脚》《最后一个冬日》《天下粮仓》《追星星的人》《爸爸去哪儿》等在此取景拍摄，进一步提升了黄河石林的知名度。

The Yellow River Stone Forest Scenic Area

9.1.1　Twenty-two Turns 二十二道弯

Twenty-two Turns, one of the most iconic features of the scenic area, is the only access to the Yellow River Stone Forest and Longwan Village. The road, with a steep wall on one side and a dizzy precipice on the other, makes it possible for tourists to appreciate both the majesty and magnificence of the Yellow River and the uniqueness and mystery of the stone forest.

Stretching 2.3 kilometers in length and descending 216 meters from the top to the bottom, Twenty-two Turns is built against the cliffs and resembles a giant dragon winding its way down the mountain. Along the journey, visitors will pass through 22 hairpin bends, each more breathtaking than the last. The nerve-shaking yet spectacular road provides an adventuresome and thrilling experience that is truly unforgettable.

二十二道弯不仅是通往黄河石林和龙湾村的唯一通道，更是一处令人叹为观止的景点。沿着这条险峻的公路，游客们有机会欣赏到黄河的雄伟与壮丽，同时也能领略到石林的奇特与神秘。

Twenty-two Turns

二十二道弯依山而建，宛若一条巨龙盘绕在山腰间。其全长2.3千米，共有22道急弯，垂直落差达到216米，看起来甚是壮观。每一位来到这里的游客都会被这条公路所带来的惊险与刺激深深折服。

9.1.2　Yinma Canyon 饮马沟大峡谷

The 4.5-kilometer-long Yinma(Horse-watering)Canyon is the first scenic spot opened up in the Yellow River Stone Forest Scenic Area. Legend has it that Genghis Khan(1162–1227), the founder and Great Khan(emperor)of the Mongol Empire, once watered horses here. Hence the name.

In the canyon stand a great many towering stone pillars, the heights of which range from 80 to 100 meters with the tallest reaching over 200 meters. They are in various lifelike shapes, named as "A Thousand Sails", "Elephants Playing in Water", "Lovers in Moonlight", "A Lion Guarding the Pass", etc. With its unique geological formations and dramatic landscapes, Yinma Canyon is also a popular filming location for many movies and television works, such as *The Myth* and *Mulan*.

A Thousand Sails

饮马沟大峡谷是黄河石林景区开发最早的景点，谷内纵深达4.5千米。相传，成吉思汗当年征战时曾在此饮马，因而得名"饮马沟"。

饮马沟峡谷内峰林耸立，石柱大多高达80至100米，最高的石柱甚至超过200米。峡谷中的岩石造型千姿百态、栩栩如生，如"千帆竞发""大象戏水""月下情侣""雄狮当关"等，这些自然造型惟妙惟肖，让人叹为观止。《神话》《花木兰》等众多影视作品曾在此取景拍摄。

9.1.3 Waterwheel 黄河水车

There are two meters-high waterwheels standing along the Yellow River in the scenic area, easily visible from the Observation Deck. Modeled on the antique waterwheel, they are another highlight of the scenic area.

Waterwheel, also called "Giant Wheel", "Lifting Wheel" or "Tiger Wheel", is a famous ancient Chinese invention, which can be traced back to the Ming Dynasty (1368–1644). It was used to irrigate fields for centuries.

The principle of waterwheel is simple yet full of wisdom. The center of the waterwheel is placed with an axle and boards. The outer bound of the wheel is fixed with a series of buckets. As the flowing water drives the wheel, the lower buckets fill with water. When the buckets pass the top of the wheel, the water is poured into a trough, which then channels the water to irrigate fields.

Waterwheel

从黄河石林景区的观景台上，游客可以远远望见两架矗立于黄河岸边的水车。它们依照古代水车的样式建造，成为景区中的一大热门景观。水车是中国明代的一项伟大发明，又称"天车""灌车""老虎车"，曾是古人用来取水灌溉农田的重要工具。

水车的设计原理虽然简单，却蕴含着古人的智慧。水车的中心装有车轴和木板，水斗被安装在水车的外缘。当流动的河水推动水车缓缓转动时，水斗便随之舀满河水。随着水车的转动，当水斗行过顶部时，水会自动倾倒入水槽之中，随后被输送至农田进行灌溉。

9.1.4　Sheepskin Raft 羊皮筏子

Sheepskin raft, as the name suggests, is made of sheepskins. When a sheep is killed, the locals remove the skin and make an airbag out of it through a meticulous process, including heating to remove hair, soaking in salty oil, drying and blowing. A raft usually consists of 9–12 sheepskin airbags. Owing to the low cost and great convenience, it was widely used as a major means of transportation for people living along the Yellow River, China's second longest river, in ancient times.

Nowadays, the sheepskin raft has evolved from a practical tool to a unique tourist experience. Drifting on the oldest ferry tool along the Yellow River, tourists can not only enjoy the stunning views along the river from a different perspective, but also experience a novel sensation of floating gently with the current.

Tourists Ride Sheepskin Rafts on the Yellow River

　　羊皮筏子顾名思义是由羊皮制作而成。当地人杀羊后剥下羊皮，经过脱毛、浸油、晾晒、充气等工序，将其制成气囊状。一个羊皮筏子通常由9～12个这样的皮囊组成。羊皮筏子因成本低廉，使用便利，在古代成为黄河上主要的渡河工具。

　　如今，羊皮筏子已成为黄河石林景区的一大旅游特色。游客坐着羊皮筏子顺流而下，不仅可以欣赏到沿途的壮丽风景，还能体验到"随波逐流"的独特乐趣。

9.1.5　Donkey Taxi 驴的

　　It's a 9 kilometers' round trip from Yinma Canyon, one of the major tourist attractions in the scenic area, to the foot of the Observation Deck. Given this distance, donkey taxis, therefore, are the most convenient and enjoyable mode of transportation for sightseers to tour the scenic zone.

　　While journeying through the grand landscapes along the way on donkey taxis, tourists can learn the local history and culture through the tales and anecdotes shared by the drivers, which not only greatly enhances the enjoyment of the trip but also deepens their understanding of the region's rich heritage.

Donkey Taxi

饮马沟至观景台脚下来回共计9千米路程，距离相对较远。因此，驴的成为游客游览黄河石林最好的代步工具。

坐在驴车上，游客不仅可以悠闲地穿梭在黄河石林的壮丽景色之中，还能聆听老乡讲述当地的奇闻轶事，这为他们提供了一个深入了解当地历史文化的宝贵机会。

9.2 Yongtai Ancient Fort 永泰古城

Located in Sitan, Jingtai, 25 kilometers from the county seat, Yongtai Ancient Fort is also known as Yongtai Turtle Fort as its shape is like a turtle. It's one of the most representative and best - preserved military buildings of the Ming Dynasty(1368–1644)along the ancient Silk Road. In 2006, it was listed as a key heritage site under state protection.

The ancient fort was built by the Ming government to defend against northern nomadic invaders. The construction of the fort began in 1607 (the 35th year of Wanli in the Ming Dynasty)and was completed a year later. It covers an area of approximately 318 *mu*, and its 12 - meter high walls form a turtle - shaped fort that is 520 meters long and 460 meters wide. Features such as barbicans, moats and bacon towers made it highly efficient for defense. Yue Zhongqi(1686–1754), a famous senior general in the Qing Dynasty(1616–1912), was once stationed here. In recent years, local authorities have been devoted to renovating the walls and relics in a bid to restore their original looks.

Yongtai Ancient Fort has become a landmark for local cultural tourism, attracting a large number of tourists from home and abroad to visit and explore. It's also a popular filming location. Many movies and television works have been shot here, such as *Mulan*, *Welcome To Sha - ma Town*, *The Last Winter Day* and *The Western Hot Spot*, which have further promoted its reputation.

　　永泰古城坐落于景泰县寺滩乡，距县城25千米，因其外形如龟，又称永泰龟城。作为丝绸之路沿线现存最具代表性且保存比较完整的明代军事建筑之一，永泰古城于2006年被列为全国重点文物保护单位。

　　永泰古城始建于明万历三十五年（1607），并于次年竣工，城池墙高12米，长520米，宽460米，占地面积约318亩，是当时明政府为防御北方游牧部落入侵而修建的军事城堡。城中建有瓮城、护城河、烽火台等设施，防御功能强大。清代名将岳钟琪（1686—1754）曾驻扎于此。近年来，当地政府一直致力于修复文物和城墙，以恢复古城的原始风貌。

　　如今，永泰古城已成为当地文化旅游的热门景点，每年吸引大量国内外游客前来参观游览。这里也是诸多影视作品的取景拍摄地。《花木兰》《决战刹马镇》《最后一个冬日》《西部热土》等在此成功拍摄，使得永泰古城的知名度得到了进一步的提升。

An Aerial View of Yongtai Ancient Fort

Yongtai Elementary School 永泰小学

　　In the fort stands a century-old elementary school named Yongtai Elementary School, which was founded in the ninth year of the Republic of China (1920) by Li Shanche, a native of Yongtai. This Gothic building skillfully blends the best parts of the architectural characters of China and the West. Known as a "book‑shaped school", it faces south and features a rational and exquisite design with bilateral symmetry.

Yongtai Elementary School is one of the three best‑preserved elementary schools built in the period of the Republic of China. It stands as "a living fossil" that witnessed the development of China's modern elementary education. Unfortunately, it was officially closed in 2014 as the majority of the residents relocated and the number of students declined sharply.

永泰古城内有一所拥有百年历史的小学——永泰小学。该校由永泰人李善澈于民国九年（1920）创建，是一座中西结合的哥特式建筑。学校坐北朝南，布局合理，设计精巧，以中轴线对称展开，左右对称，因此也被称为"一本书"校园。

永泰小学是目前全国保存较为完好的三所民国时期小学之一，是见证中国近代初级教育发展历程的"活化石"。然而，随着居民外迁，学生数量锐减，永泰小学于2014年正式停止办学。

Yongtai Elementary School

9.3 Wufo Temple 五佛寺

Wufo Temple, also known as the Temple of Five Buddhas, is located in the east of Jingtai and on the west bank of the Yellow River, approximately 20 kilometers away from the county seat. It's a key cultural relics unit under provincial protection. Legend has it that in the Northern Wei Dynasty (386– 534), a group of monks stopped off in Wufo on their way to Qinghai to build the Ta'er Lamasery. They all dreamed of five living Buddhas descending from heaven, which inspired them to build Wufo Temple.

Within the temple lies a renowned grotto known as Yansi Grotto. It's 9 meters deep and 7 meters wide, housing five giant Buddhist statues and 1,000 small ones. All the statues look stately, graceful and are really true to life. Built 1,500 years ago, the grotto is one of the earliest and best-preserved historical monuments in Jingtai.

Fronting water and backed by hills, Wufo temple has a dense growth of evergreen trees, and boasts a long history and brilliant culture, making it a great alternative for sightseeing and a holy and sacred place for Buddhist worship.

A temple fair is held annually on the eighth day of the fourth lunar month, which is the birthday of Buddha. On this day, pilgrims from far and near flock to the temple to worship Buddhas and pray for blessings. The temple fair features a wide range of religious and cultural events, offering people a great chance to appreciate folk arts and experience traditional culture. Besides, fair-goers can enjoy delicious local snacks, buy fresh farm produce and pick up exquisite handicrafts. Going to the temple fair has become a tradition for Jingtai people.

五佛寺位于景泰县东部、黄河西岸，距离景泰县城20千米，是省级重点文物保护单位。相传在北魏年间，一众僧人前往青海修建塔尔寺，途经五佛乡时在此短暂休息。夜间，僧人们共同梦见五尊活佛从天而降，随后便就地修建了五佛寺。

　　著名的沿寺石窟坐落于五佛寺内，石窟深9米，宽7米，内有大佛五尊、小佛千尊，是景泰县最早且保存最为完好的历史古迹之一。

　　五佛寺依山傍水，苍松翠柏，绿树成荫，集自然风光与历史文化于一体，是观光游览的好去处，也是朝山礼佛的圣地。

　　每年农历四月初八是五佛寺的庙会日，届时香客络绎不绝。同时，这里还会举行多种宗教、文化活动。人们既可以欣赏当地民间艺术，感受传统文化，还可以品尝当地风味小吃，购买农特产品和手工艺品。如今，参加五佛寺庙会已成为当地人的传统。

Yansi Grotto

Wufo Temple

9.4 National Saltmarsh Wetland Park of Baidunzi 白墩子盐沼国家湿地公园

Wild Birds in the National Saltmarsh Wetland Park of Baidunzi

Situated in Shangshawo，Jingtai and on the southern fringe of the Tengger Desert，the National Saltmarsh Wetland Park of Baidunzi occupies an area of around 2,700 hectares with a distance of around 6 kilometers from east to west and 12 kilometers from north to south. It's the largest seasonal saltmarsh in the region.

The wetland park used to be a salt pond famous for its high - quality salt production. The salt industry was quite prosperous. However，with the rise of the underground water level，the low - lying area gradually turned into a large - scale saltmarsh.

Today, the wetland park plays a vital role in regulating the local climate，improving the ecological environment and conserving the biodiversity. It's also a great place for bird watching, offering bird - lovers an exciting encounter with a wide range of wild birds. As a key hub on the Central Asian - Indian flyway of migratory birds, it has grown into a paradise for birds in recent years， with a large number of migratory birds, including some species listed as national rare and precious animals, attracted to nest and breed here.

September and October are the best time to enjoy the captivating beauty of the wetland park. As the sun begins to set in the west, tourists will definitely be astonished by an extraordinary oil-painting-like scenery just like what Wangbo, a well-known poet of the Tang Dynasty(618-907), wrote in his Preface to Tengwang Pavillion, "The evening glow parallels with a solitary duck to fly; the autumn river shares a scenic hue with the vast sky."

白墩子盐沼国家湿地公园位于景泰县上沙沃镇，地处腾格里沙漠南缘。公园占地面积约2700公顷，东西长约6千米，南北宽约12千米，是景泰县最大的季节性咸水沼泽湿地。

这片湿地公园原为当地著名的盐池。然而，随着地下水位的上升，这片低凹区域逐渐变成了如今颇具规模的咸水沼泽。

白墩子盐沼国家湿地公园在调节当地气候、改善生态环境、保护生物多样性等方面发挥着至关重要的作用。这里还是中亚—印度候鸟迁徙路线上的重要驿站。近年来，包括许多国家珍稀物种在内的大量候鸟纷纷来此繁衍生息，使其成为鸟儿的天堂，以及绝佳的观鸟胜地。

The National Saltmarsh Wetland Park of Baidunzi Meets the Sky at Sunset

每年9月、10月是这里最美的季节。每当夕阳西下，落日余晖洒在水面上，与归家的鸟儿相互映衬，呈现出王勃笔下"落霞与孤鹜齐飞，秋水共长天一色"的绝美画卷，令游人如痴如醉、流连忘返。

9.5 Ruins of Suoqiao Ancient Ferry 索桥古渡遗址

The Ruins of Suoqiao Ancient Ferry are located north of Suoqiao Village in Luyang, approximately 20 kilometers away from the county seat. Suoqiao Ancient Ferry was originally built in the Han Dynasty（202 BC–220 AD），connecting Jingtai on the western bank of the Yellow River with Jingyuan on the opposite side. It once served as a vital access on the Silk Road to the Western Regions，witnessing the heyday of commerce along the ancient Silk Road. In ancient times，it was crowded with merchants and camel trains，and trade was prosperous.

Ruins of Suoqiao Ancient Ferry

Literature shows that wooden boats and sheepskin rafts were the main means of transport to cross the Yellow River in the region. In the 29th year of Wanli (1601) in the Ming Dynasty (1368–1644), a floating bridge was built here to help people pass over. It was made up of 24 big boats tied up by ropes and chains.

The Ruins of Suoqiao Ancient Ferry offer a perfect blend of the cultures of the Yellow River, the Great Wall and the Silk Road. Just 300 meters downstream of the ferry lies the starting point of the Ming Great Wall west of the Yellow River. The Ming Great Wall, also called the Border Wall, in Jingtai was built in the 27th year of Wanli in the Ming Dynasty (1599) to defend against the nomadic invasions from the north. It stretches 69.3 kilometers from Suoqiao Ancient Ferry in the east to Wangjiadun in the west, with a total of 5 forts and 101 beacon towers along the way.

Over time, the once-prosperous ferry gradually fell into ruin. Only the remains tell visitors the stories of the rise and fall of the ancient ferry.

Ruins of Suoqiao Ancient Ferry

索桥古渡遗址位于芦阳镇索桥村北面，距景泰县城约20千米处。索桥古渡始建于汉代，古时是丝绸之路上连接景泰和靖远两县的重要渡口，也是内地通往西域的必经之路和商贸驿站，昔日的车水马龙、商贾云集、贸易繁荣在这里留下了深刻的印记。

　　据史料记载，这里最初以木船和羊皮筏子作为渡河工具，直至明万历二十九年（1601），政府在此修建索桥，河面上排列24只大船，用草绳将船连接成桥。

　　黄河文化、丝路文化和长城文化在索桥古渡交相辉映。古渡下游300米处是黄河以西明长城的起始处。景泰县境内明长城始建于明万历二十七年（1599），东起黄河索桥渡口，西至王家墩，全长69.3千米，沿途设有关堡5个、烽火台101座。

　　随着历史的变迁，曾经繁盛一时的索桥渡口逐渐没落。如今，只有残存的遗迹向游客们静静地诉说着往昔的辉煌与沧桑。

9.6 National Forest Park of Mount Shoulu 寿鹿山国家森林公园

　　Known as "a green island in Gobi desert", the National Forest Park of Mount Shoulu is located at the intersection of Gansu Province, Ningxia Hui Autonomous Region and Inner Mongolia Autonomous Region, and stands in the transitional zone between the Tengger Desert and the Loess Plateau, about 39 kilometers away from the county seat of Jingtai. Covering a total area of 1,086 hectares with a forest coverage of 35.2 percent and the highest peak reaching 3,321 meters above the sea level, the forest park boasts dense primeval forests, precious historical relics, beautiful natural landscapes, abundant biological resources and a pleasant climate. It's one of the areas with the highest concentration of negative oxygen ions and a popular summer resort in Jingtai.

　　Mount Shoulu, historically known as Mount Laoye or Mount Tiger, has long been a mountain of historical and cultural significance. Archaeological findings suggest that there were human inhabitants in the region as early as 4,500 years ago. The plaque of "Mount Shoulu" on the entrance gate was inscribed by Zhao Puchu, the former president of the Buddhist Association of China. The calligraphy is elegant, natural, and characterized by powerful strokes.

Mount Shoulu has distinct and captivating scenery throughout the four seasons. In spring, as the cold winter fades away, the mount is blanketed with blossoming flowers and lush trees, filling the air with fragrant scents. During summer, it becomes an ideal retreat from the summer heat. The dense forests provide shade and the gentle breezes bring relief. Autumn is the most beautiful season here. The leaves turn into red, yellow and orange, painting the mount in vibrant colors. Winter transforms the mount into a magical wonderland. The trees are covered with a white blanket of snow and the whole mount becomes a peaceful and serene place. Moreover, Mount Shoulu is rich in Taoism culture. There are many magnificent Taoist temples.

Deer in the National Forest Park of Mount Shoulu

寿鹿山国家森林公园位于甘、宁、内蒙古三省（区）交会处，地处腾格里沙漠与黄土高原的过渡地带，距景泰县城39千米，被人们誉为"戈壁绿岛"。公园总占地面积达1086公顷，森林覆盖率为35.2%，最高峰海拔3321米。这里森林繁茂、古迹众多、风景如画、生物资源丰富、气候宜人，是人们理想的避暑胜地和天然氧吧。

　　寿鹿山旧称老爷山、老虎山，自古便是景泰的历史文化名山。考古发现，早在4500年前，这里就已经有人类活动。山门牌楼上"寿鹿山"三个大字为原中国佛教协会会长赵朴初先生亲笔题写，字体端正大方，气势刚健有力。

　　寿鹿山四季分明，景色各异。春天，花团锦簇、香气四溢；夏天，绿树成荫、清风送爽；秋天，万紫千红、层林尽染；冬天，白雪皑皑、银装素裹。除了令人陶醉的自然景观，寿鹿山还是道教文化的圣地。山上建有众多道教建筑，庄严肃穆，气势恢宏。

The Entrance Gate of Mount Shoulu

9.7 Mount Wutong 梧桐山

Mount Wutong is located in Sanyanjing Village, Shangshawo, around 25 kilometers away from the county seat. There still exist a number of Euphrates poplar trees. These thousand-year-old trees are weather-beaten but still thriving. As autumn arrives, the leaves begin to fade from dark green to yellow before settling into a radiant golden amber, forming a poetic picture.

Legend has it that the mount was once densely covered with phoenix trees and phoenixes nested and lived here, so it was also called Mount Jifeng. "Jifeng" literally means "the gathering of phoenixes". Not far from the phoenix trees stood a high platform called Luofengtai, which was said to be a resting spot for the phoenixes.

Mount Wutong has been recognized as a holy and sacred site since ancient times. There are both Taoist temples and Buddhist temples. When you reach the peak, the breathtaking scenery unfolds before your eyes, so spectacular that it feels as if you were in a fairyland.

Mount Wutong

Euphrates Poplar Trees

梧桐山位于上沙沃镇三眼井村，海拔2000米，距景泰县城约25千米。梧桐山上生长着许多历经千年风雨的胡杨树，这些古树虽已饱经风霜，却依然枝繁叶茂，展现出顽强的生命力。每年秋天，胡杨叶子开始从深绿色变为黄色，然后变成琥珀色，为梧桐山披上了一层迷人的秋装。

相传古时，山上长满了郁郁葱葱的梧桐树，引得凤凰栖息于此，因此这里又被称为集凤山。在距离梧桐林不远的地方有一高台，名为落凤台，传说是凤凰休息的地方。

梧桐山上道观和佛殿交相辉映，是名副其实的仙佛同山。登上梧桐山主峰，放眼望去，壮丽的景色尽收眼底，如诗如画，宛若仙境，让人心旷神怡。

9.8 Xifan Caves 西番窑

Xifan Caves are located in Sanhe Village, Zhongquan, around 50 kilometers away from the county seat. The caves, with a history of over 1,200 years, are seen as one of the most significant archaeological discoveries of the 21st century in Gansu Province. Sanhe Village was listed as a Chinese Traditional

Village in 2014.

The caves are interconnected and have 112 front openings with a total internal floor area of around 3,430 square meters. The largest cave covers an area of 600 square meters while the smallest is just 3 square meters. Literature shows that the caves were built as dwellings by the Tubo people, who occupied the region in 764 and lived there for nearly 90 years.

Xifan Caves were of great significance in the history of Chinese revolution. In October 1936, the Fifth, Ninth and Thirtieth Armies of the Fourth Front Red Army crossed the Yellow River at Hubaokou in Jingyuan and arrived at Xifan Caves, where they took a short rest and held important meetings. The caves also played a vital role in helping the locals defend against bandits and floods in the past.

Xifan Caves

西番窑位于中泉镇三合村，距景泰县城约50千米，拥有超过1200年的悠久历史，是21世纪甘肃考古工作的一项重大发现。三合村于2014年被列入"中国传统村落名录"。

西番窑内部结构复杂，四通八达，有正面洞口112孔，洞内总面积约3430平方米。其中，最大的洞内面积达到600平方米，最小的仅3平方米。据史料记载，公元764年，吐蕃人占领此地，并在这里繁衍生息近90年。为解决住宿问题，他们修建了这些窑洞。

西蕃窑在中国革命史上发挥了重要作用。1936年10月，红四方面军的第五军、九军和三十军从靖远虎豹口渡过黄河后来到西蕃窑，在此进行了短暂休整，并召开了重要会议。此外，在历史上，西番窑在帮助当地群众抵御土匪、躲避洪灾等方面也扮演了重要角色。

9.9 Honggou Danxia 红沟丹霞

Known as "a wonder of nature", Honggou Danxia is one of the most beautiful and picturesque landscapes in Jingtai. It's situated in Yaoshui, Zhongquan, 10 kilometers away from the Yellow River Stone Forest Scenic Area and 50 kilometers from the county seat. Covering an area of around 4 square kilometers, this site stretches 1.2 kilometers from north to south and 3.2 kilometers from east to west. This unique landform was formed 4 million years ago as a result of collective forces of gravity collapse, rain erosion, weathering, etc.

Honggou Danxia, similar to Zhangye Danxia which is renowned for its layers of colorful sandstone, features vibrant colors and intricate formations. There are various shapes of high cliffs, peaks and hills, such as "Roc Spreading Wings", "Golden Toad Gazing At Moon", "Lion Holding Head High", "Dragon Soaring From Sea", "Turtle Looking Back" and "Tiger Dashing Down Mountain". Shaped by Mother Nature, all of them are lifelike and magnificent, fully presenting the majestic and grand scenery typical of northwestern

China.

　　红沟丹霞位于景泰县中泉镇腰水村，距黄河石林风景区仅10千米，距景泰县城50千米，南北宽1.2千米，东西长3.2千米，面积约4平方千米，是景泰县最具代表性的自然景观之一。红沟丹霞是大自然历经约400万年雕琢而成的杰作，其形成过程是重力崩塌、雨水溶蚀、风力侵蚀等多种自然力量共同作用的结果。

The Magnificent View of Colorful Danxia Landforms in Zhongquan，Jingtai

红沟丹霞色彩鲜艳，结构复杂。这里地貌造型奇特且形态各异，其中"鲲鹏展翅""金蟾望月""雄狮昂首""蛟龙出海""金龟回首""猛虎下山"等自然造型神形兼备、栩栩如生、气势磅礴，充分展现了中国西北地区雄浑粗犷的自然风光，堪称大自然的鬼斧神工，令人叹为观止。

9.10 Shuanglong Temple 双龙寺

Covering an area of 10 *mu*, Shuanglong Temple (Double Dragon Temple), formerly known as Biyun Temple, is situated in Luyang. As one of the grandest and most influential temples in Jingtai, it boasts a long history and distinctive architectural features.

Shuanglong Temple

Legend has it that the temple was initially built by Biyun, a Zen master in the Ming Dynasty (1368–1644). It was originally named Biyun Temple after the Zen master, and later renamed Shuanglong Temple. The Mahavira Hall (Da Xiong Bao Dian) was restored in the 29th year of Guangxu of the Qing Dynasty (1903) and extensions were made during the years of the Republic of China. A statue of Sakyamuni, the founder of Buddhism, stands meters high in the Mahavira Hall, giving a compassionate and stately appearance. Every year on the eighth day of the fourth lunar month, the birthday of Buddha, pilgrims of all ages and genders come here in groups to worship and pray for blessings.

Shuanglong Temple is not only a holy place of Buddhism, but also a sacred place of the Chinese revolution. In November 1936, during the Battle of Yitiaoshan, the headquarters of the West Route Army of the Chinese Workers' and Peasants' Red Army were stationed at the temple.

双龙寺，又名碧云寺，坐落于景泰县芦阳镇，是县内著名的古刹之一。双龙寺占地面积约10亩，以其悠久的历史和独特的建筑风格闻名。

双龙寺始建于明代。相传，当时有一位名叫碧云的禅师云游至此并建寺，名曰碧云寺，后更名为双龙寺。清光绪二十九年（1903），寺院重修了大雄宝殿。民国时期，双龙寺又增建了其他殿宇。大雄宝殿内塑有释迦牟尼像，佛像慈悲宝相、巍巍庄严。每年农历四月初八，当地男女老幼成群结队来双龙寺祈福。

双龙寺既是佛教圣地，也是革命圣地。1936年11月，中国工农红军西路军军部进驻双龙寺，并在此指挥了著名的一条山战役。

9.11 Shuigou Wetland Park 水沟湿地公园

Shuigou Wetland Park is located in Luyang, 15 kilometers southeast of the county seat. It integrates sightseeing, catering, amusement and fishing, providing a perfect destination for locals and tourists to get close to nature and relax.

The park not only boasts extraordinarily beautiful natural scenery but also shows harmony between humans and nature. With half of its total 700,000 square - meter area covered by water, it provides an ideal habitat for a wide range of wild animals, including many rare and endangered species. Touring the park, you can hear the gentle gurgling of water, see fish swimming at the bottom of the lake, watch children playing joyfully by the lakeside, and observe egrets flying overhead, all of which come together to create a harmonious ecological scene.

In the park stands a statue of Zhang Qian(164 BC–114 BC), a royal emissary in China's Han Dynasty (202 BC–220 AD)who traveled westward over 2,000 years ago and opened the Silk Road, a marvelous historical trade route connecting the East and the West. Legend has it that Zhang Qian once stopped off at this very area on his way to the Western Regions, adding a layer of historical significance to the park.

水沟湿地公园位于景泰县芦阳镇，距县城东南15千米。这里集观光旅游、餐饮、娱乐和垂钓于一体，是人们亲近自然、放松身心的好地方。

这里不仅自然风光秀美，同时也体现了人与自然的和谐共生。公园占地面积达70万平方米，约50%为水域，为众多野生动物提供了栖息和繁衍的家园。园内潺潺的水声、湖底畅游的鱼儿、湖边嬉戏的孩童以及头顶飞过的白鹭，共同构成了一幅美丽和谐的生态画卷。

公园内还矗立着一座汉代使节张骞的塑像。2000多年前，张骞西行开辟了连接东西方的丝绸之路。相传张骞出使西域途中曾途经此地。

Shuigou Wetland Park

9.12 Memorial Park of the Formation of the West Route Army in Jingtai 西路军景泰组成纪念园

Situated in Zhaojiashui, Zhongquan, 33 kilometers south of the county seat, the Memorial Park of the Formation of the West Route Army in Jingtai covers an area of 75,400 square meters, stretching approximately 290 meters from north to south and 260 meters from east to south. Established in 2019, the park is dedicated to promoting and preserving the revolutionary spirit of the West Route Army.

After the successful union of the three main forces of the Chinese Workers' and Peasants' Red Army in Huining, Gansu Province in October 1936, the Fifth, Ninth and Thirtieth Armies of the Fourth Front Red Army crossed the turbulent Yellow River at Hubaokou in Jingyuan and entered Jingtai. On November 8, 1936, with the approval of the Central Revolutionary Military Commission, the West Route Army of Chinese Workers' and Peasants' Red Army was officially established in Zhaojiashui, with Chen Changhao as the Chairman of the Military and Political Committee and Xu Xiangqian as the Commander-in-Chief.

The West Route Army sparked the flame of the Chinese revolution on this land, awakening the poor and conservative peasants. Local despots were overthrown and their lands were redistributed to the poor, who later voluntarily served as guides and donated necessities to support the army. Despite numerous difficulties and dangers along the way, the army and the people of Jingtai overcame them one after another, leaving behind many epic stories.

The formation of the West Route Army in Jingtai is a milestone in the history of the Long March of the Red Army, opening a new chapter in the history of the new-democratic revolution in the region. This sacred land of revolution holds precious spiritual wealth left by the revolutionary predecessors, which continues to inspire and motivate Jingtai people from generation to generation.

西路军景泰组成纪念园位于中泉镇赵家水村，距景泰县城以南33千米，总占地面积为75400平方米，南北长约290米，东西宽约260米。纪念园于2019年成立，旨在传承和保护西路军革命精神。

1936年10月，中国工农红军三大主力在甘肃省会宁县胜利会师后，红四方面军的第五军、第九军、第三十军从靖远县虎豹口渡过黄河，进入景泰地区。1936年11月8日，经中革军委批准，中国工农红军西路军在赵家水正式组建，由陈昌浩担任军政委员会主席，徐向前任前敌总指挥。

西路军在景泰这片土地上播撒下了革命火种，唤醒了贫穷、守旧的劳苦大众。他们打土豪、分田地，群众也纷纷自愿为他们当向导、捐赠物品。尽管在景泰的日子里充满艰难险阻，但西路军和景泰人民携手并肩，克服了一个又一个困难，留下了许多可歌可泣的感人故事。

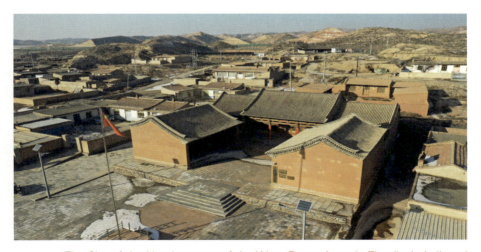

The Site of the Headquarters of the West Route Army in Zhaojiashui, Jingtai

西路军在景泰的组建是中国工农红军长征史上的重要里程碑，为景泰县新民主主义革命史揭开了崭新的一页。这片红色圣地所蕴含的革命先辈留下的宝贵精神财富，激励着一代又一代景泰儿女，成为他们心中不朽的丰碑。

9.13 Dadunhuang Film Studio 大敦煌影视城

Covering an area of 5,000 square meters, Dadunhuang Film Studio, the first film studio that reflects Dunhuang culture in China, is located in Dashuizha, Xiquan, approximately 20 kilometers east of the county seat.

The "Mogao Grottoes" in the film studio are constructed at a 1:1 scale, replicating the original Mogao Grottoes in Dunhuang. There are a total of 108 grottoes. The main grotto houses an 8.8‑meter‑high statue of Maitreya Buddha, which was sculpted by Duan Yiming, a member of the China Artists Association. The Street of the Ming and Qing Dynasties features buildings constructed in their authentic ancient styles. Walking down the street, tourists may feel as though they traveled back in time to the Ming and Qing dynasties. Additionally, there are a large number of oleaster trees and red willows, presenting a signature scenery of northwestern China.

Dadunhuang Film Studio has become a highly popular destination for filmmakers in western China. It's the location of numerous renowned films, including *The Great Dunhuang*, *Mulan*, *Snowflake Flying*, *Pretty Big Feet* and *The Myth*, attracting a large number of visitors who want to take a look at the very spot where the films were shot.

大敦煌影视城位于喜泉镇大水磁村，东距县城约20千米，占地面积达5000平方米，是中国第一家以传承和发扬敦煌文化为主题的影视拍摄基地。

影视城内的"莫高窟"按照敦煌莫高窟1∶1的比例精心建造，共有108个洞窟。其中，主窟内有一尊8.8米高的弥勒佛像，由中国美术家协会会员段一鸣先生创作而成。影视城内还建有"明清一条街"，古色古香的建筑让人们仿佛穿越时光隧道，回到了那个风华绝代的时代。此外，城内种植了大量红柳和沙枣树，充分展现出了中国西北地区的独特风貌。

大敦煌影视城已成为中国西部重要的影视拍摄基地。《大敦煌》《花木兰》《雪花那个飘》《美丽的大脚》《神话》等诸多影视作品在此成功取景拍摄，使其声名远播。

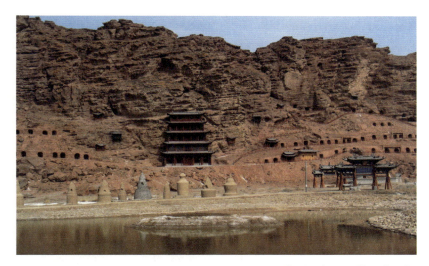

Dadunhuang Film Studio

9.14 Bolin Villa 柏林山庄

Covering an area of around 600 *mu*, Bolin Villa is located in Wufo, a township along the Yellow River that is known as "an oasis beyond the Great Wall and a land of fish and rice". The villa boasts stunning natural views. Without a glimpse of the sand dunes behind it, you might mistake it for a place south of the Yangtze River. Integrating business, leisure, catering, accommodation and entertainment, it has become a must - see for tourists who visit Jingtai.

Bolin Villa is situated at the junction where the Yellow River meets the Tengger Desert, offering visitors a rare opportunity to enjoy both the splendid desert landscape and the serene beauty of the river. They will surely be astonished by a breathtaking scenery just like what Wang Wei (701-761), one of the most famous Chinese poets of the Tang Dynasty (618-907), wrote in *On Mission to the Frontier* "In the vast desert rises straight, lonely smoke. The grand, long river reflects the round setting sun".

The scenic area has a wide range of activities on offer. Visitors can slide down the massive sand hills, ride camels, take a drive in the desert, swim and more, offering a thrilling and unforgettable experience.

Bolin Villa

柏林山庄坐落于享有"塞上江南、鱼米之乡"美誉的景泰县五佛乡，占地面积约600亩，是集商务、休闲、餐饮、娱乐、住宿于一体的观光旅游胜地。柏林山庄环境秀美，若非山庄后面的沙漠，游客甚至会误以为自己置身于江南水乡。

在这里，游人不仅能欣赏到广袤的沙漠和秀丽的黄河风光，更能感受到诗人王维笔下"大漠孤烟直，长河落日圆"的壮美景象。

景区内还为游客提供了多种体验活动，如滑沙、骑骆驼、沙漠卡丁车、游泳等，让游客在享受自然美景的同时，也能尽情体验沙漠带来的乐趣和刺激。

9.15 Xindunwan Grassland 新墩湾草原

Xindunwan Grassland, the best-preserved natural grassland in Jingtai, is situated in Sitan and at the southern foot of Mount Shoulu, 60 kilometers west of the county seat. Spanning an area of around 50 hectares, it sits at an average altitude of 2,600 meters and receives an average annual precipitation of around 200 millimeters.

Xindunwan Grassland boasts crystal-clean water, lush grass, fresh air, and pleasant climate. In summer, flocks of Tan sheep and yaks leisurely graze

Xindunwan Grassland

on the grass while Malan flowers and morning glories burst into full bloom, interspersed with a variety of other wildflowers. All these make the place appear like a natural oil painting. The grand view can be vividly depicted by a line from *The Song of Chile*, a famous Chinese poem, "Under the vast sky is the boundless wild. The wind bends the grass low, where cows and sheep show."

Xindunwan Grassland is an ideal retreat for people wanting to escape the summer heat. It not only offers tourists a chance to immerse themselves in the charm of boundless grassland, but also allows them to temporarily step away from the hustle and the bustle of urban life, finding a place for their soul to rest and achieving a deep sense of inner peace.

新墩湾草原位于景泰县寺滩乡境内，寿鹿山南麓，西距景泰县城60千米。这里海拔2600米，年降雨量约200毫米，是景泰县境内保存最为完好的天然草原，总面积约50公顷。

新墩湾草原水草丰美，空气清新，气候宜人。牛羊在草地上悠闲地觅食，马莲花与牵牛花竞相绽放，还有诸多野花点缀其间，犹如一幅大自然精心绘制的油画。人们在这里可以真切地领略到《敕勒歌》中"天苍苍，野茫茫，风吹草低见牛羊"的壮美草原风光。同时，这里也是人们炎炎夏日中理想的避暑胜地。

新墩湾草原不仅是一片让人沉醉的美丽草原景观，更能带你暂时远离城市的喧嚣，享受心灵的片刻宁静。

Yaks Graze on the Grass

9.16 Dashuizha Village 大水磋村

Adjacent to Dadunhuang Film Studio, Dashuizha Village, also known as Stone Tribe, is located in the southeast of Xiquan, Jingtai, approximately 22 kilometers away from the county seat. With the Baotou-Lanzhou Railway and Provincial Highway 201 passing through, the village enjoys a superior geographical location and prominent regional advantages. Lying between the Yellow River Stone Forest Scenic Area and Yongtai Ancient Fort, it serves as a key transit station for tourism, which integrates sightseeing, entertainment and leisure.

Dashuizha Village

As a national 3A scenic spot renowned for its abundant and uniquely shaped stones, this rural tourist destination highlights elements such as stones, water ponds, homestays, blooming flowers and film shooting. It was included in the list of China's Beautiful Leisure Villages of 2019 and the list of Top 100 Popular Check-in Spots of Gansu of 2020.

大水磅村，又称石头部落，位于景泰县喜泉镇东南部，距景泰县城约22千米。这里紧邻大敦煌影视城，包兰铁路、省道201穿村而过，地理位置优越，区位优势明显，是连接黄河石林、永泰古城，集观光、娱乐、休闲于一体的黄金旅游中转站。

大水磅村因村内石头众多、形态各异而闻名，是国家3A级旅游景区。这里成功融合了石头景观、水塘、民宿、花海和影视拍摄等元素，形成了独特的乡村旅游景点。2019年大水磅村入选"中国美丽休闲乡村"名单，2020年入选"甘肃100个网红打卡地"名单。

9.17 Huada Ski Resort 华达滑雪场

Covering an area of over 75,700 square meters, Huada Ski Resort, also known as Baiyin National Snow Sports Training Base, is located at the junction of Provincial Highway 217 and the road to the Yellow River Stone Forest Scenic Area. It is 35 kilometers from Baiyin and 50 kilometers from the county seat of Jingtai. The resort can accommodate up to 2,500 visitors at a time and has attracted over 300,000 visitors since its official opening in 2017.

Huada Ski Resort is an exceptional tourist attraction that fully integrates sightseeing, entertainment, dinning and skiing. It has five ski slopes designed for skiers of all levels, including two beginner slopes, two intermediate slopes and one advanced slope. There's also a snow entertainment area for children. Tourists can enjoy the charm and fun of winter sports through a wide range of ice-and-snow activities. With its challenging slopes, beautiful scenery, high-quality snow and well-equipped facilities, Huada Ski Resort has become a must-visit destination for winter sports enthusiasts in Jingtai.

　　白银国家雪上项目训练基地华达滑雪场坐落于省道217线与通往黄河石林景区道路的交会处，距白银市区35千米，距景泰县城50千米，占地面积约7.57万平方米，可同时接待2500余人。自2017年开业以来，该滑雪场已累计接待游客超过30万人次。

　　华达滑雪场是一个集旅游、娱乐、餐饮和滑雪运动于一体的旅游胜地。滑雪场内共建成五条雪道，包括两条初级雪道、两条中级雪道和一条高级雪道，可满足不同水平滑雪爱好者的需求。此外，滑雪场还设有儿童戏雪乐园。游客在这里可以体验到多种冰雪项目，尽情领略冬季运动的魅力与乐趣。如今，华达滑雪场凭借其充满挑战性的雪道、美丽的自然风景、优良的雪质和完善的设施，已成为当地冬季游玩的必选地。

Ski Slopes of Huada Ski Resort

10

Special Agricultural Products
特色农产品

Located in the upper reaches of the Yellow River and at the golden farming belt of 37 degrees north latitude, Jingtai enjoys unparalleled natural advantages for agricultural production. Flat terrain, fertile soil, sufficient sunshine and a big temperature difference between day and night all contribute to the exceptional quality of the agricultural products.

Jingtai has a total of 1.19 million *mu* of cultivated land, including 770, 000 *mu* of irrigated land and 420, 000 *mu* of non - irrigated land. As an important production base for commodity grain in China, Jingtai is renowned for its diverse range of special agricultural products and local brands, such as Wufo jujube, Heshangtou wheat flour, Longwan apple, watermelon, seed melon, goji berry, linseed oil, honey, Tiaoshan pear, Tiaoshan preserved apricot, etc.

景泰县位于黄河上游，地处北纬37°优质农产品黄金种植地带。这里地势平坦，土壤肥沃，光照时间长，昼夜温差大，为农作物生长提供了极为优越的自然条件，孕育出品质上乘的农产品。

景泰县拥有耕地119万亩，其中水地77万亩，旱地42万亩，是中国重要的商品粮基地。当地特色农产品丰富多样，包括五佛枣、和尚头面、龙湾苹果、西瓜、籽瓜、枸杞、胡麻油、蜂蜜、条山梨、条山杏脯等。

10.1 Wufo Jujube 五佛枣

Wufo, located along the Yellow River and known as the "Home of Red Jujubes of China", has a long history of jujube cultivation. Legend has it that in the Northern Wei Dynasty (386–534), a group of monks stopped off in Wufo on their way to Qinghai to build the Ta'er Lamasery. They dreamed of five living Buddhas coming down from heaven. Afterwards, they built Wufo Temple (Temple of Five Buddhas) and planted jujube trees there. That's where the names, Wufo (Five Buddhas) and Wofu jujube, come from. It's also said that in the Tang Dynasty (618–907), Xuanzang, one of the most famous Buddhist monks in China, passed Wufo on his journey to India to obtain Buddhist scriptures. Feeling refreshed and energetic after eating Wufo jujube, he took the pits with him and spread them to Qinghai and Xinjiang.

With its abundant sunlight, heat and water resources, Wufo produces top-quality jujubes, which feature thin skin, thick flesh, small pits, high sugar content and rich nutrition. The fresh jujubes, like tiny apples, have a sweet and crisp texture, while the dried ones are soft and moist inside with sweet smell.

Jujubes are highly valued as a food, a health supplement and a traditional Chinese medicinal herb. Their health benefits were recorded in the earliest Chinese medical classics, *Huangdi Neijing* (*Inner Canon of the Yellow Emperor*) and *Shennong Bencao Jing* (*Shennong's Classic of Materia Medica*). Wufo jujube is celebrated for its functions of tonifying qi, nourishing blood, strengthening spleen and stomach,etc.

In recent years,Wufo jujube has been highly favored by customers and the supply often fails to meet the demand.

景泰县五佛乡地处黄河之滨，以其悠久的枣树种植历史而闻名，被誉为"红枣之乡"。相传在北魏时期，有一众僧人在前往青海修建塔尔寺的途中于此地休息。当夜，众僧人梦见五尊活佛从天而降，于是他们就地修建了五佛寺，并种下了枣树，这便是五佛乡和五佛枣的由来。据说，后来唐朝高僧玄奘在取经途中经过此地，品尝五佛枣后顿感神清气爽、体力充沛，便将其带至青海、新疆地区。

五佛拥有丰富的光、热、水资源，为枣树的生长提供了得天独厚的自然条件。五佛枣以其皮薄、肉厚、核小、含糖量高和营养丰富而著称。新鲜的五佛枣口感甘甜脆爽，干枣则肉质柔软、甜而不腻。

大枣不仅是一种美味的食材，还具有滋补和药用价值。早在《黄帝内经》和《神农本草经》等中国古代医学典籍中，就记载了大枣的多种健康益处。五佛枣味道甜美，同时具有补气、活血、强脾和健胃等功效。

五佛枣凭借其卓越的品质，多年来一直深受消费者的喜爱，常常供不应求。

Wufo Jujube

10.2 Heshangtou Wheat Flour 和尚头面

Heshangtou wheat flour is milled from Heshangtou wheat, a unique wheat variety that has no awn. Mainly grown in the non-irrigated gravel land in Sitan, Jingtai, it's named for its awnless ear, which resembles the bald head of a Buddhist monk, hence the name "Heshangtou" (Head of Monk).

Today, Heshangtou wheat is still cultivated in a traditional way. The fields are not fertilized and no pesticides are used, ensuring that the flour produced is truly green and pollution-free. The protein-rich flour not only is packed with nutrients, but also is a perfect ingredient for making hand-pulled noodles, mantou (steamed buns), etc, offering them a chewy texture and distinctive taste.

Heshangtou wheat flour enjoys a high reputation in the northwest of China. Legend has it that it once served as a tribute to the royal court in the Ming and Qing dynasties.

Heshangtou Wheat

和尚头面是由和尚头麦子精心磨制而成的珍贵面粉。和尚头麦子是一种无芒小麦，主要生长在景泰县寺滩乡的旱沙地里。这种麦子麦穗无芒，形似和尚的头，故而得名"和尚头"。

当地农民至今依然沿用传统的耕种方法，不施化肥，不打农药，确保了和尚头面作为绿色无公害农产品的纯正品质。和尚头面营养丰富，蛋白质含量高，用其制作的拉条子和馒头等面食，口感筋道，风味独特，深受人们喜爱。

和尚头面在中国西北地区享有盛誉，相传在明清时期曾作为贡品供皇室享用。

10.3 Longwan Apple 龙湾苹果

As a local specialty registered as one of the National Agro-product Geographical Indications, Longwan apples are cultivated in Longwan（Dragon Bay）, a village named one of the top ten most beautiful villages in China in 2013.

With an arid climate, abundant sunlight and a large temperature difference between day and night, Longwan produces top quality apples, which are known nationwide for their pefect shape, thin peel, small core, excellent flavor and rich nutrition. The main variety is Red Fuji, which is sweet, crisp and juicy with an inviting fragrance. A single fruit weighs 220 g on average.

Longwan Apple

As the old saying goes "an apple a day keeps the doctor away", Longwan apples are highly beneficial to human health. They help relieve fatigue, improve digestion, reduce cholesterol, stabilize blood sugar levels and lower the risk of cancer.

景泰县特产龙湾苹果产自龙湾村，这里在 2013 年被评为"全国十大美丽乡村"之一，龙湾苹果也获得了全国农产品地理标志认证。

得益于当地干燥的气候、充足的光照、显著的昼夜温差，龙湾苹果形状佳、皮薄、核小、口感上乘、营养丰富。主要品种红富士，平均单果重 220 克，果实硕大、口感甘甜爽脆、多汁且香气四溢，深受消费者喜爱。

龙湾苹果不仅美味，还对健康有诸多益处，如缓解疲劳、促进消化、降低胆固醇、稳定血糖、减少癌症风险等。

10.4 Watermelon 西瓜

The cultivation of watermelons in Shili, a village in the east of Jingtai, has a history of nearly 100 years. Thanks to the arid climate, long sunlight hours, as well as a big temperature difference between day and night, the watermelons are big in size, and have thin rinds and sweet red pulp. Grown in the sandy land covered with gravel, they are also rich in selenium, one of the 14 essential trace elements that are beneficial to human health. Moreover, the watermelons are relatively firm, making them particularly suitable for long-distance transportation.

Nowadays, watermelon growing has become a pillar industry in the region. It has promoted the economic growth and lifted the locals out of poverty. In recent years, with the implementation of east-west paired assistance programs, the watermelons have been shipped to Shanghai, Tianjin, Nanjing, etc, which has further expanded the market and increased the income of local residents.

A Girl Harvests Watermelons in Jingtai

　　景泰县东部的十里村有近百年的西瓜种植历史。这里干旱的气候、充足的日照、巨大的昼夜温差以及沙砾覆盖的土壤，使得这里种出的西瓜皮薄、个大、甜度高、口感好，并且富含人体必需的微量元素——硒。此外，这里的西瓜肉质坚实，耐储存，适合长途运输。

　　如今，西瓜产业已成为当地的支柱产业，对当地的经济增长起到了关键作用，帮助当地群众摆脱了贫困。近年来，随着东西部扶贫协作的推进，十里村的西瓜已远销上海、天津、南京等地，进一步扩大了市场，提高了当地农民的收入。

10.5 Seed Melon 籽瓜

The sufficient sunlight, large temperature difference between day and night, and fertile soil rich in trace elements in Sitan provide favorable conditions for cultivating seed melons, a unique variety of watermelon. The melons, with thin rinds and rich pulp, are sweet, juicy and refreshing, making them one of the favorite winter fruits among the locals. Additionally, they offer many health benefits, such as relieving cough, eliminating phlegm and nourishing the spleen and stomach.

Seed melons get their name because of the large number of seeds they contain. Apart from the delicious pulp, the seeds are also edible and highly nutritious. Known as "black melon seeds", they are packed with plenty of nutrients, including protein, unsaturated fatty acids, dietary fiber, vitamins B and E, and a variety of minerals like magnesium, zinc, iron and potassium. They are of great benefit for good health, such as providing energy, promoting digestion, and protecting cells from free radical damage.

For their excellent quality, reasonable prices and promising marketing, the planting area for seed melons has been continually expanding over the years. It now covers more than 20,000 *mu* with an annual output exceeding 30,000 tons. Seed melons have become a "cash cow" that helps the locals lead a better life.

Seed Melons Grown in Sitan

景泰县寺滩乡光照充足、昼夜温差大、土壤肥沃，非常适宜籽瓜种植。这里产出的籽瓜皮薄肉厚、口感甜爽，是寒冷冬季人们最喜爱的瓜果之一。不仅如此，籽瓜还具有止咳祛痰、滋补脾胃的保健功效。

籽瓜因其含籽量多而得名，其籽俗称黑瓜子。黑瓜子营养丰富，含有蛋白质、不饱和脂肪酸、膳食纤维、维生素 B 和维生素 E，以及镁、锌、铁和钾等多种矿物质。这些成分对人体健康至关重要，能够提供能量、促进消化、保护细胞免受自由基损伤等。

寺滩籽瓜品质优良，价格合理，市场前景广阔。近年来，籽瓜种植面积不断扩大，目前已达到 2 万多亩，总产量超过 6000 万斤。籽瓜已成为助力当地群众过上美好生活的"摇钱树"。

10.6 Jingtai Goji Berry 景泰枸杞

Jingtai goji berries are a local specialty registered as one of the National Agro-product Geographical Indications. Thanks to its adequate sunlight, low rainfall, large temperature difference between day and night, and fertile soil, Jingtai is one of China's main goji berry-producing regions, and produces the finest goji berries. The planting area spans approximately 100,000 *mu* with an annual output of fresh goji berries reaching 250,000 tons.

Jingtai goji berries are dark red in color, large in size, thick in flesh, high in sugar and rich in nutrients. They are an excellent addition to tea, congee and soup. The berries are believed to have a wide range of health benefits, including improving sleep quality, promoting eye health, resisting aging, promoting blood circulation, supporting the immune system, preventing Alzheimer's disease and reducing the risk of cancer.

In recent years, many new varieties have been introduced in Jingtai. The local government has also worked to standardize the planting, harvesting and processing techniques while expanding the sales through promotions and setting up outlets. With more and more people embracing healthier lifestyles,

Jingtai goji berries have not only gained a high reputation in the home market，but also become increasingly popular with international consumers.

景泰枸杞是景泰县的特产，获得了全国农产品地理标志认证。景泰县是我国重要的枸杞生产基地之一。这里光照充足、降雨稀少、昼夜温差大、土壤肥沃，这些优越的自然条件共同孕育了景泰枸杞的卓越品质。目前，景泰县枸杞种植面积约10万亩，年产枸杞鲜果约25万吨。

景泰枸杞色泽偏暗红、个大、肉厚、含糖量高、营养丰富，是人们泡茶、煮粥、熬汤的不二选择。此外，景泰枸杞具有显著的保健功效，能够提高睡眠质量、保护视力、延缓衰老、促进血液循环、提高免疫能力、预防阿尔茨海默病、降低癌症风险等。

近年来，当地不仅引进枸杞新品种，还在种植、采摘和加工过程中制定严格的标准并不遗余力地进行推广。随着人们对健康生活方式的日益重视，景泰枸杞不仅在国内市场上享有盛誉，也受到了国际消费者的青睐。

Jingtai Goji Berries

10.7 Linseed Oil 胡麻油

Linseed oil is a yellowish edible vegetable oil extracted from flaxseed. It's rich in nutrition and features a distinctive taste. Moreover, it offers a variety of health benefits, including regulating fat and hormone levels, stimulating blood circulation, delaying aging and reducing the risk of cancer.

Nowadays, flax is still cultivated in a traditional way with no use of chemical fertilizers or pesticides in Jingtai, which ensures that the linseed oil produced is truly pollution-free and organic. As one of the local special agricultural products, Jingtai linseed oil is not only an ideal choice for home cooking, but also an excellent gift for relatives and friends. In recent years, it has become increasingly popular throughout the country.

胡麻油是从胡麻中压榨而成的一种食用植物油。它色泽微黄、味道独特、营养丰富，还具有多种对人体有益的保健功效。胡麻油能够调节人体脂肪和激素水平、促进血液循环、延缓衰老、降低患癌风险等。

如今，当地人依然采用传统方法种植胡麻，不施化肥，不打农药，确保所产胡麻油是纯正的绿色有机食品。景泰胡麻油作为当地的特色农产品，不仅是自家烹饪的理想选择，也是赠送亲友的绝佳礼品。近年来，景泰胡麻油在全国各地越来越受到消费者的喜爱和认可。

Jingtai Linseed Oil

10.8 Honey 蜂蜜

Situated in the upper reaches of the Yellow River and on the southern fringe of the Tengger Desert, Jingtai has favorable climate and abundant bee plants, making it an ideal region for producing one hundred percent natural honey.

The main varieties of Jingtai honey include all-flower honey, acacia honey, jujube honey, goji berry honey and so on. Rich in glucose, fructose and various vitamins and trace elements, Jingtai honey is of great benefit to human health. It helps maintain beauty, calm the nerves, reduce anxiety and build up the body. Jinghui Honey, one of the renowned local honey brands, is highly favored by customers across the country for its top-quality products and beautifully designed packaging.

景泰县地处黄河上游、腾格里沙漠南缘。这里气候适宜、蜜源植物丰富，为纯天然蜂蜜的生产提供了得天独厚的条件。

景泰蜂蜜的主要品种包括百花蜜、洋槐蜜、枣花蜜、枸杞蜜等。这些蜂蜜富含葡萄糖、果糖以及多种维生素和微量元素，不

Jinghui Honey

仅营养丰富，还具有多种保健功效，如美容养颜、安神补脑、消除焦虑和强身健体等。景泰当地的著名蜂蜜品牌"景卉"蜂蜜，凭借其纯正的品质和精美的包装，深受全国消费者的喜爱。

10.9 Tiaoshan Pear 条山梨

Jingtai has a long history of pear cultivation, which dates back to the late Ming and early Qing dynasties. The fertile soil rich in trace elements and favorable climate contribute significantly to the exceptional quality of the pears.

As a local specialty registered as one of the National Agro - product Geographical Indications, Tiaoshan pear, the main varieties of which include Zaosu pear and Huangguan pear, is juicy, crisp and sweet with a delightful aroma. As Li Shizhen, a distinguished Chinese medical scientist of the Ming Dynasty (1368–1644), noted in the *Compendium of Materia Medica* "pears are of different varieties and all are beneficial to health", Tiaoshan pear is of high medicinal value. It helps clear away heat and toxic material, relieve cough, eliminate phlegm and nourish the lung and spleen. It's widely used to soothe throat, bronchial and lung complaints. In addition, Tiaoshan pear is rich in immune - friendly vitamin C, and fiber which helps reduce cholesterol level and lower the risk of heart disease.

Tiaoshan Pear

景泰县栽种梨树历史悠久，最早可追溯至明末清初时期。当地肥沃的土壤和适宜的气候非常适宜梨的生长。

条山梨是景泰县特产之一，凭借其卓越的品质获得了全国农产品地理标志认证。目前，条山梨的主栽品种包括早酥梨和黄冠梨，其口感香甜、爽脆、多汁。李时珍曾在《本草纲目》中写道："梨品甚多，俱为上品，可以治病。"条山梨不仅美味，而且药用价值很高，具有清热解毒、止咳化痰、滋养肺脾等功效，被广泛用于缓解喉咙、支气管和肺部疾病。此外，条山梨富含有助于提升人体免疫力的维生素C和有助于降低胆固醇和患心脏病风险的纤维素。

10.10 Tiaoshan Preserved Apricot 条山杏脯

With the Yellow River in the east, the Qilian Mountains in the west, and the Tengger Desert in the north, Tiaoshan Farm produces top-quality apricots thanks to long sunlight hours and a large temperature difference between day and night. Tiaoshan preserved apricot is made of Dajie apricot from the farm, an apricot variety unique to Gansu Province. The ripe Dajie apricot is large in size with thick flesh. A single fruit weighs 150 g on average.

Tiaoshan preserved apricot tastes sweet and slightly sour with the original flavor. It's rich in glucose and fructose, which are easily absorbed by the body. This combination of distinctive flavor and nutritional value has made the preserved apricot highly popular among consumers across the country.

Tiaoshan Preserved Apricot

条山农场东临黄河，西依祁连山，北与腾格里沙漠毗邻，日照时间长，昼夜温差大，为杏子生长提供了得天独厚的自然条件。条山杏脯选用条山农场种植的大接杏为原料制作而成。这种杏子个大肉厚，单果平均重量可达150克。

条山杏脯完美保留了杏子的天然风味，甜中带酸，口感独特。它富含葡萄糖和果糖，这些糖分极易被人体吸收，营养价值高。如今，条山杏脯在全国市场上广受欢迎，成为众多消费者的喜爱之选。

11

A Taste of Jingtai 景泰美食

As a popular tourist destination along the Silk Road, Jingtai not only boasts numerous historical relics and various landscapes, but also is home to a great many delicacies, making it a paradise for food lovers.

Some of the must-try delicacies include Wofo tofu, Dawan fish, Mafu baozi, Suanlanrou, Jingtai lamb meat, Sanfan, Hand-pulled noodles, Jiaotuan, Multi-layer cake, Minced pork noodles, Niangpi, Huidouzi, Shacong salad, Pickled Chinese cabbage, Suet mush, Huidou noodles, Sweet oats, etc.

景泰县作为丝绸之路上的旅游重镇，不仅以其丰富的历史遗迹和多样的自然风光吸引着游客，更以其琳琅满目的美食让人流连忘返。

景泰特色美食主要包括五佛豆腐、大碗鱼、麻腐包子、酸烂肉、景泰羊羔肉、糁饭、拉条子、搅团、千层饼、臊子面、酿皮、灰豆子、凉拌沙葱、酸菜、油茶、灰豆饭、甜醅子等。

11.1 Wufo Tofu 五佛豆腐

Wufo tofu, a typical local delicacy, boasts a history spanning over 200 years and can be traced back to the Qing Dynasty (1616–1912). The yellowish tofu is renowned for its particular ingredients and unique tofu-making techniques. It offers an unparalleled taste and texture. With an inviting aroma, it tastes light, natural and incredibly delicious. Every bite is satisfying. In addition, Wufo tofu is celebrated for its nutritional benefits. It's low in calories, high in protein and contains essential amino acids, vitamins and minerals, making it a great choice for health-conscious foodies.

Today, Wufo tofu has evolved from a less-known local dish to a special treat for guests from far and wide, enjoying a great reputation both in the region and beyond.

Wufo Tofu

五佛豆腐是当地的传统美食，起源于清朝，至今已有200多年历史。五佛豆腐色泽微黄，用料讲究，制作方法独特。其浓郁的香气和清淡、自然、美味的口感，让人每一口都能感受到深深的满足。此外，五佛豆腐热量低、蛋白质含量高，富含有人体必需的氨基酸、维生素和矿物质，是追求健康饮食者的绝佳选择。

如今，五佛豆腐声名远播，已从昔日鲜为人知的地方小吃变成了宴请宾客的上佳菜肴。

11.2 Dawan Fish 大碗鱼

Dawan（Big Bowl）fish is one of the iconic dishes in Jingtai cuisine. It gets the name because it's always served in a big bowl. It's nutritious and delicious, and leaves a delightful and lasting aftertaste.

Dawan fish gains a high reputation for its distinctive ingredient—the Yellow River carp. The fish are raised in the ponds whose water is a mixture of the water from the Yellow River and the saline groundwater, making them particularly rich in nutrition and have a superior flavor. Cooked together with Wufo tofu, garlic stem and cilantro, the fish is more tender and palatable. Autumn and winter are the golden seasons for enjoying Dawan fish.

Dawan Fish

大碗鱼因用大碗盛鱼而得名，是景泰县久负盛名的一道美食，以其营养丰富、味道鲜美、回味悠长而备受赞誉。

大碗鱼的主要食材是黄河鲤鱼，其生长在由黄河水与地下盐碱水混合而成的鱼塘中。独特的水质赋予了鲤鱼更高的营养价值和更鲜美的口感。搭配上五佛豆腐、蒜苗和香菜，大碗鱼鲜嫩可口、美味无比。秋冬季节是品尝大碗鱼的黄金时节。

11.3 Mafu Baozi 麻腐包子

Mafu baozi is another well-known local delicacy in Jingtai. The filling is quite distinctive. It's mainly made of boiled diced potatoes mixed with mafu, a special ingredient made from hemp seeds. With rich nutrition, Mafu baozi is fluffy and has a fresh and delicious taste that satisfies both the locals and the visitors seeking an authentic taste of Jingtai.

In Jingtai, there is a tradition of eating Mafu baozi on the Winter Clothing Day, a traditional Chinese memorial day that falls on the first day of the tenth lunar month. It marks the arrival of cold winter and serves as a reminder to provide warmth and comfort to one's ancestors. On this day, people burn offerings, such as paper money and paper clothes, to honor their ancestors and commemorate deceased family members.

Mafu Baozi

麻腐包子是景泰的特色美食。其馅儿制作考究，是将优质的土豆切丁煮熟后与麻腐混合搅拌而成。麻腐包子质地松软、味道鲜美、营养丰富。无论是当地人，还是寻求景泰味道的外地游客，麻腐包子都会给你带来愉快而难忘的美食体验。

在景泰，人们有在寒衣节吃麻腐包子的习俗。寒衣节是中国传统的祭祀节日，每年农历十月初一，人们都会祭扫烧献，纪念逝去的亲人。

11.4 Suanlanrou 酸烂肉

Suanlanrou is a classic homemade dish that is quite popular among the locals. It's cooked mainly with pork, pickled cabbage and vermicelli. The meat is fat but not greasy, offering a rich flavor. The pickled cabbage, made of fresh Chinese cabbage, tastes sour, crispy and highly appetizing. The potato starch-made vermicelli is chewy and springy. Together, they create a unique taste that is simply irreplaceable. Suanlanrou goes best with Sanfan.

All the natives, no matter where they are or how many delicacies they have tasted before, will find that a plate of Suanlanrou is always the one that can truly satisfy their stomachs and warm their hearts.

Suanlanrou

酸烂肉是景泰当地的传统家常菜，由猪肉、酸菜和粉条三种食材共同烹制而成。肥而不腻的猪肉，酸脆开胃的酸菜，嚼劲十足的粉条，三者完美结合，造就了酸烂肉独一无二的风味，令人回味无穷。酸烂肉搭配糁饭，味道绝佳，深受人们喜爱。

对于景泰人来说，无论他们身处何地，尝过多少山珍海味，总是会发现没什么佳肴能比一盘酸烂肉更能让自己身心满足。

11.5 Jingtai Lamb Meat 景泰羊羔肉

Jingtai has a deep-rooted culture of eating mutton throughout the year, especially in the cold seasons. There are many popular ways to cook mutton, such as boiling, braising, frying, grilling, etc.

Jingtai lamb meat is a legendary dish in the region, mainly sourced from lambs raised in Cuiliu. These lambs graze in the mountains where there are a wide range of medicinal herbs and many mineral-rich springs. Thus they are referred to as "green animals" that feast on medicinal herbs and drink mineral water.

Jingtai lamb meat is fat yet not greasy, tender and juicy with no unpleasant odour. It's particularly rich in nutrition and has numerous health benefits, such as strengthening the immune system, promoting blood circulation, dispelling cold, removing dampness, invigorating spleen and supplementing qi.

Jingtai Lamb Meat

景泰人对羊肉总是情有独钟，烹饪方法也是多种多样，从清炖到红烧，从爆炒到烧烤。

景泰羊羔肉是当地餐桌上的一道经典美食，其原料主要来自翠柳地区放牧的羊羔。这些羊羔生长在得天独厚的自然环境中，以山上丰富的中草药为食，饮用富含矿物质的山泉水。因此，翠柳羊羔被誉为吃着中药草料、喝着山泉水长大的"绿色动物"。

景泰羊羔肉以其肉质肥而不腻、鲜嫩多汁、无膻味而闻名。它不仅口感上乘，而且营养价值丰富，具有增强人体免疫系统、促进血液循环、驱寒祛湿、健脾益气等功效。

11.6 Sanfan 糁饭

Sanfan is a popular local delicacy with a long history that can be traced back to the Tang Dynasty(618−907).

The process of making Sanfan is simple but requires great patience. The recipe is like this: Place clean rice in a pot with an appropriate amount of water. Boil the rice until it is medium - well. Sprinkle a little amount of wheat flour, around one-fifth the amount of the rice, evenly over the rice and leave it to simmer for another 15 minutes. Stir the rice and flour constantly until they are thoroughly mixed. Stirring is the key part to make perfect Sanfan, just as the saying goes: 360 stirs make a good Sanfan.

Sanfan

Sanfan smells inviting and tastes soft and chewy. It's one of the staples for the locals. It's said that with a bowl of Sanfan, you can go for a whole day without eating anything else. The locals love to enjoy it with a plate of Suanlanrou, creating a perfect combination of flavors.

糁饭是当地历史悠久的传统美食，其历史渊源可追溯至唐代。

制作糁饭的过程虽不复杂，但却需要极大的耐心。首先，将米淘洗干净后下锅，待熟至七八成时，均匀撒上面粉，盖上锅盖再焖一刻钟。随后，便是关键的搅拌过程，正如当地俗语所说"糁饭若要好，三百六十搅"。这一步需要不断地搅拌，直至米与面完全融合。

糁饭是景泰人餐桌上的主食之一，以其出锅时扑鼻的饭香和软中带劲的口感而备受人们喜爱。它不仅耐饥饿，搭配上酸烂肉一起食用，更是味道绝佳，令人回味无穷。

11.7 Hand-pulled Noodles 拉条子

Hand-pulled noodles, also known as Latiaozi, are composed of noodles stretched by hands, fresh vegetables and top quality pork. With a smooth and chewy texture, the noodles are an exceptionally delicious and satisfying dish.

Hand-pulled Noodles

Hand-pulled noodles play a significant role in the local food culture. For Jingtai people, the taste of home is just a plate of steaming hand-pulled noodles, which are seen as one of the most scrumptious and comforting foods in the world. Whenever thinking of this delicacy, they couldn't help seeking out the special taste deeply rooted in their minds, even if they are far away from home. If you ever visit Jingtai, trying Hand-pulled noodles isn't just about tasting a dish—it's a bite of the region's history and culture.

拉条子是景泰地区著名的面食，由手工拉制的面条、新鲜蔬菜和精选猪肉共同烹制而成，凭借其爽滑筋道的口感和无与伦比的美味深受人们喜爱。

拉条子在当地饮食文化中占据着重要位置。对于当地人而言，家的味道就是一盘热气腾腾的拉条子，这被视为他们心中最美味的食物。无论他们走到哪里，对这一口的执念始终没有变。只要想到拉条子，就会抑制不住想要寻找那深深扎根于内心深处的美味。如果您有机会去景泰，品尝拉条子不仅仅是享受一道美食，更是在感受当地的历史与文化。

11.8 Jiaotuan 搅团

Jiaotuan, a delicacy typical to Jingtai that is usually made of potatoes and wheat flour, always awakens deep memories of taste with its unique charm.

The process of making Jiaotuan is not complicated yet requires great patience. First, potatoes are diced and boiled until they are medium-well. At this point, sprinkle an appropriate amount of wheat flour evenly over them. When both the potatoes and the flour are well-done, stir the mixture in the same direction constantly until it becomes pasty with no lumps. Then place it on a plate and leave it to cool.

Jiaotuan, which looks like white jade, is sticky, springy and incredibly delicious. It's traditionally served with Saozi soup (minced pork soup), pickled leek, vinegar and mashed garlic. It pleases the eyes, nose and palate of the eaters.

搅团是用土豆和面粉制作而成的景泰特色美食，总能以其独特的魅力唤醒人们味蕾深处的记忆。

搅团的制作过程并不复杂，但需要十足的耐心。首先，将土豆切成小丁，放入沸水中煮至七分熟。接着，均匀地撒入小麦面粉，继续煮至土豆和面粉熟透。之后，朝同一方向不停搅拌，直到没有任何结块，完全变成糊状。最后，将其盛入盘中，冷却凝固成团即可。

搅团外观洁白如玉，质地黏稠而富有弹性，吃起来既劲道又美味。搭配上臊子汤、腌韭菜、醋和蒜泥等调料，更是色香味俱佳，让人回味无穷。

Jiaotuan

11.9 Multi-layer Cake 千层饼

Multi-layer Cake

The multi-layer cake, also known as thousand-layer cake, is an indispensable food in Jingtai during the Mid-Autumn Festival, which is celebrated on the fifteenth day of the eighth lunar month. In the days leading up to the festival, the residents in Hongshui and neighboring towns usually busy themselves preparing the distinctive moon cake. This tradition has been practiced for generations. In the past, people would place little patterns of rabbits made of dough on the top of the cakes, embodying their longing for family reunions. The multi-layer cake is not only enjoyed at family gatherings at the Mid-Autumn Festival but also serves as a popular gift for relatives and friends.

Nowadays, with more local delicacies brought to market, the layered cake, featuring appealing color and distinctive flavor, is becoming increasingly popular and is frequently served on various occasions.

千层饼是当地人在中秋节必备的传统美食。每逢中秋佳节，红水镇及周边地区的人们便会忙碌起来，开始制作这一独特的月饼。在过去，人们还会在千层饼上精心摆放用面捏成的小兔子，来寄托他们对家人团圆的美好愿望。千层饼不仅是自家享用的美味，也是中秋佳节馈赠亲朋好友的上佳礼品。

如今，随着当地特色美食文化的传播，千层饼凭借其色泽诱人、口味独特的特点，越来越受到人们的喜爱，成为餐桌上的一道亮丽风景。

11.10 Minced Pork Noodles 臊子面

Minced Pork Noodles

Minced pork noodles, originating from the Longevity Noodles of the Tang Dynasty（618-907）, are one of the locals' favorites. The noodles are thin, smooth and chewy, while the soup, consisting of a variety of ingredients such as diced toufu, diced potatoes and minced pork, is good in color, aroma and taste. Together, they create a taste that is out of this world.

Minced pork noodles are a special treat that the locals always serve for their guests during festivals. All the local residents, men and women, old and young, take great delight in eating the noodles and the taste lingers on for a long time.

Moreover, the noodles have gone beyond food to become a cultural symbol in Jingtai. Having it on festive occasions, like weddings, festivals and birthdays, is a traditional practice with special meanings. For example, eating Minced pork noodles on one's birthday is considered as a wish for a long and healthy life.

臊子面起源于唐代的长寿面，是景泰人最钟爱的美食之一。其面条细滑、口感独特且富有嚼劲，而由豆腐、土豆、猪肉等多种精选食材精心烹饪而成的臊子汤，更是色泽诱人、香气扑鼻、味道浓郁。面条与臊子汤的完美结合，创造出臊子面无与伦比的美味。

在景泰，臊子面是逢年过节招待亲朋好友的主食。它凭借香浓的味道和悠长的回味，深受男女老少的喜爱。

此外，臊子面不仅是日常餐桌上的美味佳肴，还承载着特殊的文化寓意。在婚礼、节日、生日等喜庆场合，它更是不可或缺的一部分。例如，生日时吃一碗臊子面，寓意着身体健康、长命百岁，寄托着人们美好的愿望。

11.11 Niangpi酿皮

Niangpi

Niangpi, or Rangpi in the local dialect, is a popular local snack made from wheat flour. Cut into long strips and served with mustard, mashed garlic, chili oil, vinegar and soy sauce, it boasts tempting color, tender texture and savory taste. Every bite is satisfying.

Niangpi holds a special place in the hearts of Jingtai people. In the past, as summer arrived, the cries of street vendors selling Niangpi could always be heard from the street. Children would eagerly drag their parents out to buy this mouthwatering treat. It has become a cherished memory for Jingtai people, which will forever be etched in their minds.

Today, Niangpi can be found everywhere in Jingtai all year round, from fancy restaurants to street stalls. There's always a high demand in hot summer.

酿皮由面粉制作而成，是景泰著名的风味小吃。其色泽诱人，质地柔软而富有弹性，配以芥末、蒜泥、辣子油、醋和酱等调料后，每一口都是难以言喻的美味。

酿皮在景泰人心中占据着特殊的位置。在过去的夏日，每当院外传来酿皮的叫卖声，孩子们便会迫不及待地拉着家人，争先恐后地去购买。那一声声叫卖也成为许多人心中遥远而珍贵的记忆。

如今，酿皮在景泰的街头巷尾随处可见，或小摊，或酒店。尤其在炎热的夏季，酿皮更是成为一道供不应求的消暑佳肴。

11.12 Huidouzi 灰豆子

Huidouzi, a local dessert, is a delectable congee enjoying great popularity among the locals. Made of peas, penghui (an edible alkali extracted from pengpengcao, a plant native to the region), jujubes and rock candy, Huidouzi is named for its distinctive greyish color. It boasts numerous health benefits, including nourishing blood, calming nerves, and tonifying the stomach and spleen. Moreover, it has a good effect on indigestion.

With its sweet, refreshing taste and fragrant flavor from jujubes,

Huidouzi is rich in nutrition and suitable for people of all ages. It's especially popular during the summer months for its function of relieving heat. Nowadays, Huidouzi is available in almost every corner of Jingtai, from street stalls to fancy restaurants.

Huidouzi

灰豆子是用豌豆、蓬灰（从当地的蓬蓬草中提炼出的食用碱）、大枣、冰糖等食材精心熬煮而成的一种甜品粥。因为熬制好的豆子呈现出灰色，所以被称为"灰豆子"。灰豆子具有补血、安神、养胃、补脾、促消化等功效，深受人们的喜爱。

灰豆子不仅香甜爽口，且营养丰富，适合各个年龄段的人群食用，是人们炎炎夏日中的解暑佳品。在景泰的大街小巷，人们随处可见这道传统美食。

11.13 Shacong Salad 凉拌沙葱

Shacong salad is a beloved cold dish among the locals and a must-try delicacy for visitors to Jingtai. Shacong(sand onion)is a drought-tolerant vegetable that grows in desert. The root can survive three consecutive years of drought. Containing a variety of vitamins, trace elements and minerals, it's of great benefit for good health. Shacong salad, with an exceptional taste, is appetizing, refreshing and beneficial for the spleen.

The preparation of Shacong salad is easy to follow. First, wash Shacong thoroughly and boil it for a few minutes. Then, soak it in cold water for a short time to retain its crispness. Finally, remove it into a plate and season with salt, vinegar and sesame oil before serving.

凉拌沙葱是景泰老百姓钟爱的一道凉菜，也是外地游客来景泰必尝的一道美食。沙葱生长在沙漠里，生命力顽强，即使连续三年干旱，它的根也不会枯死。此外，沙葱富含多种维生素、微量元素和矿物质，为这道凉菜增添了健康价值。凉拌沙葱口味独特，具有开胃、提神、健脾的功效。

凉拌沙葱烹饪方法简单易行：先将沙葱用水淘洗数遍，放入沸水中焯烫至熟，然后放入凉水中浸泡片刻后捞出，以保持脆嫩口感。最后，加入盐、醋、香油等各种调料，即可食用。

Shacong Salad

11.14 Pickled Chinese Cabbage 酸菜

Pickled Chinese Cabbage

Pickled Chinese cabbage, an indispensable winter delicacy in Jingtai, is yellowish in color and is loved for its unique flavor and health benefits. It helps clear away heat and aid digestion.

As winter arrives, there is a tradition of preparing pickled Chinese cabbage in Jingtai. This practice can be traced back to the time when fresh vegetables were scarce and expensive during the cold months, and people needed to preserve vegetables for the winter. The recipe is as follows: First, select fresh Chinese cabbages, wash them thoroughly and cut into strips. Then, add an appropriate amount of salt, Huajiao pepper and ginger slices. Finally, place it into a clean crock, and weigh it down with a large stone. In about two weeks, it will be ready to enjoy. Cooked with pork and vermicelli, it becomes even more satisfying.

在寒冷的冬季，酸菜是景泰人餐桌上不可或缺的一道美食。其色泽淡黄，味道独特，具有清热祛火、助消化的功效，从而深受人们喜爱。

过去，冬季新鲜蔬菜极为稀缺且价格昂贵，腌制酸菜成为人们应对蔬菜匮乏的重要方式。如今，景泰家家户户每到冬天依然会腌一坛酸菜。其腌制方法简单易行，首先挑选新鲜的大白菜，将其洗净后切成条状，撒上适量食盐、花椒和生姜片等，然后装进干净的大缸中，最后在上面压一块大石头，两周后就可以食用了。搭配猪肉和粉条一起烹饪，味道绝佳。

11.15 Suet Mush 油茶

Suet Mush

The locals often have Suet mush for breakfast. It's rich in flavor yet not greasy. Moreover, it's highly nutritious and is considered as a great health food for building a strong body, particularly beneficial for sickly people.

The main ingredients of Suet mush are suet and wheat flour. Several steps are involved in making perfect Suet mush. First, heat wheat flour in an aluminum pot until it turns yellow, and remove it into a plate. Next, melt the suet, then mix in the flour and stir constantly until well mixed. Finally, add seasonings like huajiao pepper, salt, gourmet powder, etc. It will condense into chunks after cooling, thus it's less likely to go bad.

景泰人的清晨常常被一碗香气四溢的油茶唤醒。这道传统美食以味美而不腻、营养丰富、强身健体的特性，成为景泰人早餐中的宠儿。

尤其对于体弱多病者来说，油茶是极好的保健食品。

　　景泰人的油茶原料简单却讲究，主要为羊油和面粉。制作时，先将面放入锅中，炒至黄色后盛出。接着将羊油放入锅内，待其完全融化后，再将炒好的面粉倒入锅中，用铲子不停搅拌，使油和面均匀混合。最后加入花椒、盐、味精等调味品，油茶便制作完成了。油茶冷却后会凝结成块状，这样不易变质。

11.16 Huidou Noodles 灰豆饭

Huidou Noodles

Huidou noodles, also known as Hongdou noodles because of its reddish soup, are one of the locals' favorite noodles. Lentils, the main ingredient, are particularly rich in protein, vitamins and minerals. This not only makes Huidou noodles unique in taste and highly nutritious but also provides a variety of health benefits, such as clearing away heat and neutralizing stomach acid.

　　The recipe for Huidou noodles is as follows: Wash the lentils and boil them for about ten minutes. Add an appropriate amount of dietary alkali and continue boiling until the soup turns reddish brown. While preparing the soup, roll out the prepared dough and cut into thin strips. Cook the noodles in the lentil soup for around ten minutes, then season with salt and huajiao pepper before serving. Paired with home - made Pickled Chinese cabbage, it becomes an even more delicious meal.

　　灰豆饭是景泰人最喜欢吃的面食之一，因其汤色为红褐色，民间亦称其为"红豆饭"。其主要食材扁豆含有大量的蛋白质、维生素和矿物质，这不仅让灰豆饭口感独特、营养丰富，还赋予了它清热去火、中和胃酸的功效。

　　制作灰豆饭时，先将扁豆淘洗干净，放入开水中煮约十分钟，接着，加入适量食用碱，继续煮至汤变成酱红色。与此同时，将和好的面切成细长条，放入灰豆汤中再煮十分钟左右。最后，加入盐、花椒等调料就可以食用。用腌制的酸菜和咸韭菜作佐菜，灰豆饭的味道更加鲜美。

11.17 Sweet Oats 甜醅子

Sweet Oats

Sweet oats, also known as Tianpeizi, are a traditional fermented snack with a long history in Jingtai. The main ingredient is naked oats, a grain widely recognized for its high nutritional value. This special snack tastes fresh and sweet with a slight aroma of wine.

Sweet oats, deeply favored by the locals, are usually brewed around the Dragon Boat Festival, also called the Double Fifth Festival, which is celebrated on the fifth day of the fifth lunar month to commemorate Qu Yuan (340 BC–278 BC), a well-known Chinese poet and minister of the State of Chu during the Warring States Period (475 BC–221 BC). The refreshing snack can not only help relieve the summer heat but also awaken a deep sense of homesickness among Jingtai people who are far from home.

　　甜醅子，作为景泰县的传统特色小吃，承载着深厚的历史底蕴。甜醅子的主要原料是被公认为具有高营养价值的莜麦。这道风味小吃以其鲜甜的口感和淡淡的酒香而闻名，余味悠长，令人回味无穷。

　　在景泰，每逢端午节前后，家家户户都会制作甜醅子，这既是一道传统的节令美食，也是消暑解热的佳品。它不仅帮助人们在炎炎夏日中找到一丝清凉，更在无形中唤起了无数景泰游子对家乡的深深思念。

12

Jingtaichuan Electric Pumping Irrigation Project 景泰川电力提灌工程

Located on the southern fringe of the Tengger Desert, Jingtai was once a water scarce county where the residents lived in extreme poverty due to the harsh environment. To alleviate drought and improve agricultural conditions in the region, the Gansu Provincial Committee of the Party and the Provincial Government officially launched the Jingtaichuan Electric Pumping Irrigation Project, also known as the "first in China", on October 15, 1969.

The Jingtaichuan Electric Pumping Irrigation Project, also called the Jing Dian Project, is a large‑scale, multi‑provincial pumping irrigation project characterized by high lift, large flow rate and multiple stages. It is designed to lift water from the Yellow River to higher‑altitude regions. The project consists of three main parts: Phase I, Phase II and the Extension of Phase II, also known as the Min Diao Project. It includes a total of 43 pumping stations. Originally designed with a flow rate of 28.6 cubic meters per second and an increased flow rate of 33 cubic meters per second, it had an installed capacity of 259,700 kilowatts and a designed irrigation area of 824,700 *mu*. After renovations and upgrades, the design flow rate has been increased to 37.4 cubic meters per second, with an increased flow rate of 43.89 cubic meters per second, an installed capacity of 306,000 kilowatts, and a designed irrigation area of 1,145,700 *mu*. The irrigated areas cover Jingtai County, Gulang County, Minqin County and Alxa Left Banner. The long water delivery pipeline, stretching like a giant dragon winding among mountains, is truly a magnificent sight.

The construction of Phase I of the Jingtaichuan Electric Pumping Irrigation Project was completed in 1974. It includes 13 pumping stations, achieving a total lift of 472 meters. Originally designed with a flow rate of 10.6 cubic meters per second and an increased flow of 12 cubic meters per second, the project had an installed capacity of 67,000 kilowatts and a designed irrigation area of 304,200 *mu*. After extensive renovations and upgrades, the design flow rate has been increased to 13.17 cubic meters per second, with an increased flow rate of 15.8 cubic meters per second. The installed capacity is 89,000 kilowatts, and the actual irrigation area covers 331,200 *mu*. The project was led by Li Peifu (1912−1983), who, despite being in his late fifties, worked together with engineers from various backgrounds, trekking over mountains to conduct field surveys and overcoming numerous challenges. The completion of Phase I had far - reaching significance for promoting the agricultural development in central Gansu and provided invaluable experience for the construction of other irrigation projects in the following decades.

The construction of Phase II began in July 1984 and took ten years to complete. It includes 30 pumping stations, achieving a total lift of 713 meters. The original designed flow rate was 18 cubic meters per second, with an increased flow rate of 21 cubic meters per second, an installed capacity of 192,500 kilowatts, and a designed irrigation area of 520,500 *mu*. After renovations and upgrades, the designed flow rate has been increased to 24.23 cubic meters per second, with an increased flow rate of 28.09 cubic meters per second. The installed capacity is 217,000 kilowatts, and the actual irrigation area covers 645,400 *mu*. Since its completion, the project has tremendously improved the living conditions of hundreds of thousands of people across the irrigated area and has effectively prevented the desert from encroaching on the region.

The construction of the Extension of Phase II, also known as the Min Diao Project, began in 1995 and was completed in 2000, with a designed flow rate of 6 cubic meters per second. This water division project channels water from the Yellow River to Minqin County, which is located between the Badain Jaran and the Tengger—two large deserts in China covering 87,000 square kilometers in total. It has been playing a crucial role in controlling desertification and improving the ecology and people's livelihood in the county.

The Jingtaichuan Electric Pumping Irrigation Project stands as a milestone in China's decades-long efforts to combat drought. It has been a vital guarantee for the well-being and prosperity of residents in the irrigated areas. The project has completely transformed agricultural production conditions in the region and significantly improved the ecological environment. The once barren land has now become a green ecological barrier on the southern fringe of the Tengger Desert, showcasing the power of human ingenuity and perseverance in overcoming natural challenges.

The First Pumping Station of the Jingtaichuan Electric Pumping Irrigation Project

景泰县位于腾格里沙漠南缘，历史上长期面临干旱缺水的困境，这使得当地群众的生活极度贫困。为有效缓解干旱、改善农业生产条件，甘肃省委省政府于1969年10月15日启动了景泰川电力提灌工程的建设，该工程被誉为"中华之最"。

　　景泰川电力提灌工程（景电工程）是一项跨省区、高扬程、大流量、多梯级的提水灌溉工程，由一期、二期和二期延伸工程（民调工程）组成，建有43座泵站。该工程旨在将黄河水提升到海拔较高的地区。工程原设计流量28.6立方米/秒，加大流量33立方米/秒，装机容量25.97万千瓦，设计灌溉面积82.47万亩。工程更新改造后，设计流量37.4立方米/秒，加大流量43.89立方米/秒，装机容量30.6万千瓦，设计灌溉面积114.57万亩。其灌区横跨甘肃、内蒙古两省（区）的景泰、古浪、民勤、阿拉善左旗四县（旗）。输水管道宛若巨龙，在崇山峻岭之中穿行，景象十分壮观。

　　景电一期工程于1974年竣工，建成泵站13座，总扬程472米。工程原设计流量10.6立方米/秒，加大流量12立方米/秒，装机容量6.7万千瓦，设计灌溉面积30.42万亩。工程更新改造后，设计流量13.17立方米/秒，加大流量15.8立方米/秒，装机容量8.9万千瓦，实际灌溉面积33.12万亩。景电一期工程由李培福领导主持建设。当时他虽已年近花甲，但仍与工程师们一起翻山越岭、长途跋涉，对实地进行细致勘察，并克服了许多艰巨的挑战。该工程对推动甘肃中部地区的农业产业发展具有深远意义，同时也为此后几十年里其他灌溉工程的建设积累了宝贵的经验。

The Sculpture of the Jingtaichun Electric Pumping Irrigation Project

景电二期工程于1984年7月开工建设，1994年完工，建成泵站30座，总扬程713米。工程原设计流量18立方米/秒，加大流量21立方米/秒，装机容量19.25万千瓦，设计灌溉面积52.05万亩。工程更新改造后，设计流量24.23立方米/秒，加大流量28.09立方米/秒，装机容量21.7万千瓦，实际灌溉面积64.54万亩。二期工程的建成不仅显著改善了灌区群众的生活条件，还有效抵御了沙漠的侵蚀。

二期延伸工程（民调工程）于1995年启动建设，2000年竣工，设计流量6立方米/秒。该工程旨在向被巴丹吉林沙漠和腾格里沙漠包围的民勤县供水，在控制沙漠化、改善生态环境和提高当地群众生活水平方面起到了至关重要的作用。

景泰川电力提灌工程是中国几十年来与干旱斗争过程中的一个里程碑。它为灌区百姓富足生活提供了重要保障，彻底改变了当地农业生产条件，显著改善了当地生态环境，使整个灌区成为腾格里沙漠南缘一道重要的生态屏障，展现了人类在克服自然挑战方面的智慧和毅力。

Li Peifu 李培福

Li Peifu is a household name in Jingtai. The locals affectionately call him "Li Laohan" as a sign of deep respect.

Li Peifu was born in a poor peasant family in Huachi, Gansu in 1912. He joined the Red Army guerrillas in 1933 and became a member of the Communist Party of China the following year. When Li attended the Senior Officials' Meeting of the Northwest Bureau of the CPC Central Committee in Yan'an, Shaanxi in 1943, Chairman Mao Zedong inscribed "Mian Xiang Qun Zhong" (Face the Masses) on his certificate of honor to praise him for remaining true to the original aspiration and serving the people wholeheartedly.

After the founding of the People's Republic of China, Li successively served as the Director of Gansu Provincial Department of Civil Affairs and the Vice Governor of Gansu Province. He was also the general director of Phase I of the Jingtaichuan Electric Pumping Irrigation Project, a life-saving project which transformed 300,000 *mu* of barren land into fertile farmland.

Li Peifu passed away at the age of 71 in 1983, leaving the people of Jingtai in deep sorrow. To commemorate his significant contributions to the region, the headquarters of the Jingtaichuan Electric Pumping Irrigation Project, along with the People's Government of Jingtai and the People's Government of Gulang erected a bronze statue of him in Jingtai in October 1994. Li will always be remembered for his sharing weal and woe with the masses and his selfless devotion to the people, which will continue to inspire Jingtai people from generation to generation.

在景泰这片土地上，李培福的名字家喻户晓，人们亲切地称他为"李老汉"。

Li Peifu

　　李培福1912年出生于甘肃省华池县一个贫苦的农民家庭。1933年，他参加了红军游击队，次年加入中国共产党。1943年，李培福在延安参加中共中央西北局高干会议时，毛主席亲自在他获奖的奖状上题写了"面向群众"四个大字，高度赞扬他不忘初心、一心为民的高尚情怀。

　　中华人民共和国成立后，李培福先后担任甘肃省民政厅厅长、甘肃省副省长等重要职务。他领导主持了景电一期工程的建设，使30万亩荒芜的戈壁滩变成了富饶的米粮川，景电一期工程被当地群众誉为"救命工程"。

　　1983年，李培福与世长辞，享年71岁。他的离世让景泰人民陷入深深的悲痛之中。为纪念李培福在景泰川的丰功伟绩，1994年10月，景电指挥部、景泰县政府和古浪县政府在景泰为他立了一座铜像。李培福的一生，是与群众同甘共苦、为人民奉献一切的一生。他的精神将永远激励着一代又一代景泰人民。

13

Towns and Townships of Jingtai
乡镇介绍

Jingtai is a vast county with a long history. It covers a total area of 5,485 square kilometers with a distance of around 84 kilometers from east to west and 102 kilometers from north to south.

Jingtai administers 8 towns (Yitiaoshan, Luyang, Xiquan, Caowotan, Hongshui, Zhenglu, Zhongquan, Shangshawo) and 3 townships (Wufo, Sitan, Manshuitan). Altogether, there are 135 administrative villages and 16 communities. 25 ethnic groups, including Han and Hui, live in harmony, with a population of 237,191 as of 2024.

景泰县历史悠久，地域辽阔，总面积达5485平方千米，东西长约84公里，南北宽约102千米。

景泰县下辖8个镇和3个乡，包括一条山镇、芦阳镇、喜泉镇、草窝滩镇、红水镇、正路镇、中泉镇、上沙沃镇，以及五佛乡、寺滩乡、漫水滩乡。全县共有135个行政村和16个社区。截至2024年，景泰县总人口为237191人，拥有25个民族，是一个多民族聚居的地区。

13.1 Yitiaoshan 一条山镇

Yitiaoshan, which literally means "a line of hills", is located in central Jingtai and stands at the east end of the Hexi Corridor, with Wufo on the east, Xiquan on the south, Sitan on the west and Caowotan on the north. It's named because there is a line of hills near its government seat. The region was a wilderness until the completion of Phase I of the Jingtaichuan Electric Pumping Irrigation Project in 1974. Since then, it has gradually developed into a modern town.

Yitiaoshan has served as the political, economic and cultural center of Jingtai since the county seat was relocated here from Luyang in 1978. It boasts a pleasant environment and convenient transportation. The residents live and work in peace and contentment.

Covering an area of approximately 139 square kilometers with a distance of around 7 kilometers from east to west and 20 kilometers from north to south, Yitiaoshan features a falt terrain, with an average altitude of 1,610 meters. The urban area occupies 5.78 square kilometers. It has short springs and autumns, hot and rainy summers, and cold and dry winters. The average annual temperature is 8.2 ℃, with an average annual sunshine duration of 2,718.3 hours and a frost-free period of 141 days. The average annual precipitation is about 184 mm, most of which occurs in July and August.

Yitiaoshan is divided into 2 administrative villages and 13 communities with a registered population of 53,080. There are 93,000 *mu* of cultivated land. The main crops are corn, Chinese medicinal crops and vegetables. The breeding industry relies mainly on raising cattle, sheep, and pigs.

一条山镇位于景泰县中部，地处河西走廊东端，东依五佛，南接

Yitiaoshan

喜泉，西邻寺滩，北连草窝滩。因镇政府驻地附近有一条山冈，故而得名。这里曾是一片荒凉的戈壁滩，随着1974年景泰川电力提灌工程一期工程的建成，逐渐发展成为一个充满生机与活力的现代化城镇。

自1978年景泰县城由芦阳迁至一条山镇以来，这里一直是全县的政治、经济、文化中心。一条山镇交通便利，环境优美，人民生活安定和谐，是景泰县的核心区域。

一条山镇镇域面积约139平方千米，东西长约7千米，南北宽约20千米，地势平坦，平均海拔1610米。城区面积为5.78平方千米。这里四季分明，春秋季节较短，夏季炎热多雨，冬季寒冷干燥。年平均气温为8.2℃，年平均日照时数达2718.3小时，无霜期为141天，年降水量为184毫米，主要集中在7月和8月。

全镇户籍人口53080人，下辖2个行政村和13个社区。全镇耕地面积为9.3万亩，主要农作物包括玉米、中药材和蔬菜。养殖业以饲养牛、羊、猪为主。

13.2 Luyang 芦阳镇

Luyang, formerly known as Lutanghu or Luyanghu, is located in the east of Jingtai and lies in the irrigated region of Phase I of the Jingtaichuan Electric Pumping Irrigation Project, with the Yellow River on the east, Zhongquan on the south, Xiquan on the southwest, Wufo on the northeast and Yitiaoshan on the northwest.

Luyang covers an area of 354 square kilometers, stretching around 20 kilometers from east to west and 18 kilometers from north to south. The terrain slopes from the southwest to the northeast, with an average altitude of 1,500 meters. Luyang receives little rainfall but has abundant sunlight. Sandstorms hit the region from time to time. The average annual temperature is 8.2 ℃, with an average annual sunshine duration of 2,725 hours and an annual rainfall of 180 mm, which mainly occurs in August, September and October.

Luyang

Luyang is a large town with a long history, brilliant culture, and rich natural resources. It plays a significant role in the history of Jingtai. In 1933, it was set as the county seat of Jingtai and served as the political, economic and cultural center of the county for 45 years until the seat was relocated to Yitiaoshan in 1978. The cultures of the Yellow River, the Great Wall and the Silk Road co-exist here. There is a batch of famous historical heritages, such as Aowei Site, Suoqiao Ancient Ferry, the Ming Great Wall and Shuanglong Temple, and many intangible cultural heritages, including the Molten Iron Fireworks, casserole-making techniques and Bark-brush painting.

The town is divided into 13 administrative villages and 1 community with a registered population of 26,797. There are 93,700 *mu* of cultivated land. The main crops grown are corn, wheat and vegetables. The breeding industry relies mainly on raising pigs and sheep. In recent years, Luyang has seen a rapid increase in the total income of the rural collective economy, laying a solid economic foundation for rural revitalization.

芦阳镇，古称芦塘湖、芦阳湖，地处景泰县东部，位于甘肃景电一期工程灌区。东临黄河，南与中泉镇毗邻，西南连喜泉镇，东北接五佛乡，西北依一条山镇。

芦阳镇的镇域面积为354平方千米，东西长约20千米，南北宽约18千米。地势呈现出西南高、东北低的特点，平均海拔1500米。该地区降水稀少、光照充足，沙尘暴天气较为常见。年平均气温8.2 ℃，年平均日照时数2725小时，年降水量180毫米，主要集中在8—10月。

芦阳镇地域辽阔，历史悠久，文化底蕴深厚，自然资源丰富。1933年至1978年，芦阳曾是景泰县城所在地，45年间一直是全县的政治、经济、文化中心，在景泰历史上有着举足轻重的地位。黄河文化、长城文化、丝路文化在这里交相辉映，境内有媪围古城、索桥古渡、明代长城、双龙寺等丰富的历史遗产，还有打铁花、砂锅制作、树皮笔画等多个非物质文化遗产。

全镇下辖13个行政村和1个社区，户籍人口26797人，耕地面积
9.37万亩。农业以种植玉米、小麦、蔬菜为主，养殖业以饲养猪、羊为
主。近年来，全镇农村集体经济收入快速增长，为乡村振兴战略的实
施奠定了坚实基础。

13.3 Xiquan 喜泉镇

As the "south gate" of Jingtai, Xiquan is located in the southern Jingtai
and stands in the irrigated region of Phase I of the Jingtaichuan Electric
Pumping Irrigation Project, with Luyang on the east, Zhenglu on the west,
Zhongquan on the south and Yitiaoshan on the north. Archaeological findings
in the region suggest that human inhabited the area as early as 4,500 years
ago. Today, Xiquan is a suburban town with convenient transportation, boom-
ing economy and rich natural resources. The Baotou - Lanzhou Railway, the
Wuhai - Maqin Expressway and Provincial Highway 201 pass through the
town.

Xiquan covers an area of 545 square kilometers. The terrain is higher in
the southwest and lower in the northeast, with an average altitude of 1,700
meters. It experiences four distinctive seasons, with hot summers and cold
winters. The temperature varies greatly between day and night. The average
annual temperature is 8.6 ℃ with a frost-free period of 140 days and an annual rainfall of 200 mm, which mainly occurs in July and August.

The town is divided into 17 administrative villages with a registered population of 23,173. There are 2 provincial-level demonstration villages for rural construction, where the residents live in peace and contentment. Xiquan
has 117,000 *mu* of cultivated land, mainly used for growing corn, wheat, Chinese medicinal crops and vegetables. The breeding industry focuses mainly
on raising pigs, cattle and sheep.

Xiquan also boasts rich tourism resources. Dadunhuang Film Studio and

Dashuizha Village welcome a great number of tourists every year.

　　喜泉镇地处景泰县南部，位于甘肃省景电一期工程灌区，是景泰县的"南大门"。东连芦阳镇，西邻正路镇，南接中泉镇，北靠一条山镇。境内出土的文物表明，早在4500年前，这里就有人类居住生活。如今，喜泉镇交通便利，商贸繁华，自然资源丰富，包兰铁路、乌玛高速、201省道等重要交通线路穿境而过。

　　喜泉镇镇域面积545平方千米，地势西南高而东北低，平均海拔1700米。这里四季分明，冬季寒冷，夏季炎热，昼夜温差大，年平均气温8.6℃，无霜期140天，年降水量200毫米，主要集中在7、8月份。

　　全镇下辖17个行政村，总户籍人口为23173人，其中2个村被评为省级乡村建设示范村，居民生活安定，幸福感强。全镇耕地面积为11.7万亩，农业以种植玉米、小麦、中药材、蔬菜为主，养殖业以饲养猪、牛、羊为主。

　　喜泉镇不仅农业发达，而且旅游资源丰富，拥有大敦煌影视城、石头部落等多个著名景点，每年吸引大量游客前来参观游览。

Dashuizha Village

13.4 Caowotan 草窝滩镇

Caowotan is located in the north of Jingtai and lies in the junction of Gansu Province, Ningxia Hui Autonomous Region and Inner Mongolia Autonomous Region, with Wufo on the east, Yitiaoshan on the south, Sitan on the west and Shangshawo on the northwest. It enjoys convenient transportation, with the Baotou-Lanzhou Railway, the Lianyungang-Khorgos Expressway and National Highway 338 passing through.

Caowotan covers an area of 549 square kilometers. It has four distinctive seasons with short springs and autumns, hot and rainy summers, and cold and dry winters. The average annual temperature is 8.6 ℃, with an average annual sunshine duration of 2,718.3 hours. The average annual precipitation is approximately 184 mm, with the majority occurring in July and August.

The town is divided into 18 administrative villages, with a registered population of 21,601. There are 67,000 *mu* of cultivated land. The main agricultural products include goji berries, tomatoes, wheat and corn. The tomatoes gain a good reputation for the high quality and are sold in markets across major cities, such as Beijing, Shanghai and Xi'an. The goji berries received gold medals at the 7th and 10th China International Agricultural Trade Fair. The breeding industry relies mainly on raising goats, pigs and laying hens. In addition, Caowotan is rich in mineral resources, such as coal, clay and aggregates. In recent years, it has seen a big rise in the per capita income.

草窝滩镇位于景泰县北部，地处甘肃、宁夏、内蒙古三省（区）交界处，东与五佛乡毗邻，南连一条山镇，西邻寺滩乡，西北接上沙沃镇。包兰铁路、连霍高速、G338线等重要交通干线穿境而过，交通优势明显。

草窝滩镇镇域面积549平方千米，气候四季分明，春秋较短，夏季炎热多雨，冬季寒冷干燥。年平均气温为8.6℃，年平均日照时数为2718.3小时，年降水量约184毫米，主要集中在7月和8月。

全镇现下辖18个行政村，总户籍人口21601人，耕地面积6.7万亩。农业以种植枸杞、西红柿、小麦、玉米为主。其中，西红柿远销北京、上海、西安等大城市，枸杞更是荣获第七届、第十届中国国际农产品交易会金奖，享誉国内外。养殖业以饲养山羊、生猪、蛋鸡为主。草窝滩镇不仅农业发达，矿产资源也十分丰富，拥有煤炭、黏土、砂石料等多种矿产资源。近年来，全镇人均收入提升显著。

A Villager Picks Goji Berries in Xihe Village，Caowotan

13.5 Hongshui 红水镇

Located in the northwest of Jingtai, on the southern fringe of the Tengger Desert and at the boundary between Gansu Province and Inner Mongolia Autonomous Region, Hongshui serves as the northwest gate of Jingtai with Alxa Left Banner on the east, Mount Changling on the west, Manshuitan on the south and Gulang on the north. Named after Hongshui River in the region, it's an agricultural town with convenient transportation, and rich mineral resources.

Hongshui covers an area of 320 square kilometers. The terrain is higher in the southwest and lower in the northeast. It enjoys an average annual temperature of 8℃, with an average annual sunshine duration of 2,725.5 hours and an frost - free period of 178 days. The average annual precipitation is around 190 mm.

Hongshui is a town where Hui and Han ethnic groups live in harmony. It's divided into 15 villages and 1 community with a registered population of 19,576. There are 120,000 *mu* of cultivated land. The main crops grown here are corn and wheat. The locally renowned fruits include red cherries and Zaosu pears. The breeding industry relies mainly on raising pigs, cattle, sheep, chickens, donkeys and camels.

红水镇地处景泰县西北部，位于腾格里沙漠南缘，是甘肃省与内蒙古自治区的交界之地。东接阿拉善左旗，西至长岭山，南邻漫水滩乡，北靠古浪县。红水镇因境内的红水河而得名，作为景泰县的西北门户，这里不仅是全县重要的农业产区，还拥有便捷的交通和丰富的矿产资源。

红水镇的镇域面积为320平方千米，地势呈现出西南高、东北低的特点。这里年平均气温为8 ℃，年平均日照时数为2725.5小时，无霜期为178天，年降水量约190毫米。

Onions Are Harvested in Hongshui

全镇下辖15个行政村和1个社区，户籍人口为19576人，是一个回族和汉族共居的多元文化乡镇。全镇耕地面积为12万亩，农业以种植玉米和小麦为主，特色水果包括红樱桃、绿旱酥等。养殖产业以饲养猪、牛、羊、鸡、驴、驼为主。

13.6 Zhenglu 正路镇

Zhenglu, a key node along the ancient Silk Road, is located in the southwest of Jingtai, with Xiquan on the east, Tianzhu on the west, Lanzhou New Area, the fifth state-level new area of China, on the south and Mount Tiger on the north. It covers an area of 657 square kilometers. The terrain is higher in northwest and lower in southeast, with an average altitude of 2,506 meters above sea level. The average annual temperature is 3.5 ℃ and the annual rainfall is 90−210 mm, which mainly occurs in July, August and September. Zhenglu boasts convenient transportation with the Jingtai-Zhong-chuan Airport Expressway and Provincial Highway 101 passing through.

The town is divided into 16 administrative villages, with a registered population of 18,531. There are 198,000 *mu* of cultivated land, including

20,000 *mu* of irrigated land and 178,000 *mu* of non-irrigated land. The special agricultural products, such as Heshangtou wheat flour, linseed oil and yellowhorn, are highly favored across the country. There are also 680,000 *mu* of pasture, providing a solid foundation for the development of the local stock-breeding industry. Moreover, Zhenglu is rich in mineral resources, including gold, copper and limestone.

In recent years, the local authority has been stepping up its efforts to address deficiencies in infrastructure construction, optimize the industrial structure, improve the ecological environment and push forward the rural vitalization in an all-round way to build a new Zhenglu that is prosperous, beautiful and habitable.

正路镇位于景泰县西南部，东接喜泉镇，西连天祝县，南邻兰州新区，北依老虎山。全镇总面积达657平方千米，是古丝绸之路上的重要节点。正路镇地势自西北向东南倾斜，平均海拔为2506米，年平均气温为3.5℃，年降水量介于90至210毫米之间，降水主要集中在7月、8月和9月。景中高速、省道101等重要交通干线穿境而过。

Autumn Harvest in Zhenglu

全镇下辖16个行政村，户籍人口18531人。耕地面积广阔，达19.8
万亩，其中水浇地面积2万亩，旱地17.8万亩。主要农产品和尚头面
粉、胡麻油和文冠果等在全国享有盛誉。68万亩的草场为当地畜牧业
的发展提供了广阔的空间。此外，正路镇拥有丰富的矿产资源，包括
金、铜、石灰石等。

近年来，正路镇力争补齐基础设施短板，优化产业结构布局，改
善生态环境，全面实施乡村振兴战略，着力打造一个繁荣、美丽、宜
居的新正路。

13.7 Zhongquan 中泉镇

Zhongquan is located in the southeast of Jingtai, with Pingchuan and
Jingyuan on the east, Baiyin on the south and Xiquan on the west. It covers a
total area of 960 square kilometers and has a terrain that is higher in west and
lower in east, with an average altitude of 1,600 meters. The average annual
temperature is 8.6 ℃ and the annual rainfall is 193 mm, which mainly occurs
in July and August. Zhongquan has very convenient transportation with the
Baotou-Lanzhou Railway, Provincial Highway 217 and the Zhongquan-Liuch-
uan Highway passing through.

The town is divided into 12 administrative villages with a registered
population of 15,970. There are 81,300 *mu* of cultivated land. The main
agricultural products are apples, jujubes and corn. Longwan apple enjoys a
high reputation across the country for its thin peel, small core, good flavor,
high quality and rich nutrition. The breeding industry relies mainly on raising
pigs and sheep.

Zhongquan has a rich history and culture. It's a sacred land of the Chinese revolution. The West Route Army was established in Zhaojiashui,
Zhongquan in 1936, sparking the flame of Chinese revolution on this land and

awakening the poor and conservative peasants.

The town is also a popular tourist destination featuring attractions such as the Yellow River Stone Forest Scenic Area，Xifan Caves，Honggou Danxia Landform and Huada Ski Resort， which attract thousands of tourists from home and abroad annually.

中泉镇地处景泰县东南部，东与平川区、靖远县接壤，南与白银市区毗邻，西接喜泉镇，总面积达960平方千米。中泉镇地势西高东低，平均海拔1600米，年平均气温为8.6℃，年降水量为193毫米，主要集中在7月和8月。境内交通便利，包兰铁路、省道217、中刘公路等交通干线穿境而过。

全镇现下辖12个行政村，户籍人口15970人，耕地面积8.13万亩。主要农产品包括苹果、大枣、玉米等。其中，龙湾苹果以其皮薄、核小、口感佳、品质优、营养丰富而享誉全国。养殖业以饲养猪和羊为主。

中泉镇不仅农业发达，而且历史悠久，文化底蕴深厚，是中国红色革命的圣地。1936年，西路军在赵家水正式组建，为这片土地播撒了革命火种，唤醒了贫穷守旧的劳苦大众。

Longwan Village

此外，中泉镇旅游资源丰富，拥有黄河石林风景区、西番窑、红沟丹霞、华达滑雪场等著名旅游景点，每年吸引大量国内外游客前来参观游览。

13.8 Shangshawo 上沙沃镇

Shangshawo is located in the northwest of Jingtai and stands in the intersection of Gansu Province, Ningxia Hui Autonomous Region and Inner Mongolia Autonomous Region, with Wufo on the southeast, Caowotan and Sitan on the south, Hongshui on the west, and Manshuitan and Alxa Left Banner on the north. It enjoys highly convenient transportation with the Baotou - Lanzhou Railway, National Highway 338 and Provincial Highway 308 passing through.

Covering an area of 497 square kilometers, Shangshawo features a flat terrain, with elevations ranging from 1,500 to 1,800 meters above sea level. It's hot in summer and cold in winter, with an average annual temperature of 8.3 ℃. The region enjoys abundant sunlight, averaging 2,726 hours per year. The annual rainfall is 185 mm, most of which occurs in July and August.

Shangshawo is divided into 10 administrative villages with a registered population of 9,923. There are many village - level culture squares and rural libraries, which have greatly enriched the cultural life of the residents. The town has 71,000 *mu* of cultivated land. The main crops are corn and wheat. The breeding industry focuses mainly on raising pigs and sheep. Additionally, it has abundant and various mineral resources, such as gypsum, coal and iron ore.

There are also many famous tourist attractions, like Mount Wutong and the National Saltmarsh Wetland Park of Baidunzi, which draw a great number of tourists each year. In recent years, the per capita income in Shangshawo has seen a significant increase, reflecting the area's growing prosperity and development.

上沙沃镇位于景泰县西北部，地处甘肃、宁夏、内蒙古三省（区）交界处，东南与五佛乡接壤，南邻草窝滩镇和寺滩乡，西接红水镇，北与漫水滩和阿拉善左旗相连。镇域内交通网络发达，包兰铁路、国道338线、省道308线贯穿全境。

　　上沙沃镇镇域面积为497平方千米，地势平坦，海拔在1500米至1800米之间。这里冬季寒冷、夏季炎热，年平均气温为8.3 ℃，年平均日照时数达2726小时，年降水量为185毫米，主要集中在7、8月份。

　　全镇下辖10个行政村，户籍人口9923人。近年来，镇内建成了多个村级文化活动广场和农家书屋，极大地丰富了当地居民的文化生活。全镇现有耕地7.1万亩，种植业以玉米、小麦为主，养殖业以生猪、羊为主。此外，上沙沃镇矿产资源丰富，主要矿产有石膏、煤炭和铁矿石等。

　　在旅游资源方面，上沙沃镇拥有众多特色景点，如梧桐山、白墩子盐沼国家湿地公园等，每年吸引大量游客前来观光游览。近年来，上沙沃镇人均收入有了显著增长。

The National Saltmarsh Wetland Park of Baidunzi

13.9 Wufo 五佛乡

Nestled among mountains, Wufo is located in the northeast of Jingtai, with the Yellow River on the east, Luyang on the southwest, Yitiaoshan and Caowotan on the west, and Shangshawo on the north. It's the only place in Jingtai where rice is grown, earning it the reputation of "an oasis beyond the Great Wall and a land of fish and rice".

Covering an area of 583 square kilometers, Wufo stretches approximately 30 kilometers from east to west and 25 kilometers from north to south. The terrain slopes from northwest to southeast, with elevations ranging from 1,300 to 1,800 meters above sea level. The region enjoys a temperate climate, with an average annual temperature of 10.5 ℃, an average annual sunshine duration of 2,725.5 hours and an annual rainfall of 185 mm.

Wufo has a rich history and culture. Wufo Temple built in the Northern Wei Dynasty(386–534)is one of the earliest and best-preserved temples in Jingtai. The Jingtaichuan Electric Pumping Irrigation Project, known as "first in China", has contributed enormously to the agricultural prosperity. Additionally, the Association for Promotion of Anti-Japanese Aggression of Wufo, the first mass organization against Japanese aggression in the Hexi Corridor, was founded here.

Wufo is divided into 6 administrative villages with a registered population of 17,587. There are 46,000 *mu* of cultivated land. The main crops are rice, corn, jujubes and vegetables. It's known as the "Home of Red Jujubes of China". The locally-grown jujubes feature thin skin, thick flesh, a small pit, high sugar content and rich nutrition. The total planting area for jujubes has reached 21,500 *mu* with an annual output of over 32,000 tons of fresh fruit. The breeding industry focuses mainly on pigs and sheep. Wufo is also home to many delicacies, such as Wufo tofu and Dawan fish.

五佛乡地处景泰县东北部，四面环山，东临黄河，西南与芦阳镇接壤，西与一条山、草窝滩相邻，北与上沙沃相连。这里是全县唯一生产水稻的地区，享有"塞上江南、鱼米之乡"的美誉。

五佛乡总面积达583平方千米，东西长约30千米，南北宽约25千米。地势总体呈现西北高东南低的特点，海拔在1300米至1800米之间。五佛乡年平均气温为10.5℃，年平均日照时数为2725.5小时，年降水量为185毫米。

五佛乡历史悠久，文化底蕴深厚。辖区内有始建于北魏时期的五佛寺、被誉为"中华之最"的景电工程，以及河西地区第一个群众抗日组织——"五佛抗日促进委员会"。

全乡下辖6个行政村，户籍总人口为17587人。全乡耕地面积为4.6万亩，种植业以水稻、玉米、大枣和蔬菜为主。五佛素有"红枣之乡"的美誉，五佛枣以其皮薄、肉厚、核小、含糖量高、营养丰富而闻名。目前，全乡枣树种植面积达2.15万亩，年产鲜枣3.2万吨以上。养殖业以生猪、羊为主。当地特色美食五佛豆腐和大碗鱼等，以其独特的风味深受人们喜爱。

An Aerial Drone Photo Shows a View of Wufo

13.10 Sitan 寺滩乡

Sitan is located in the west of Jingtai and at the east end of the Hexi Corridor, with Yitiaoshan and Xiquan on the east, Mount Shoulu and Zhenglu on the south, Gulang and Tianzhu on the west, and Shangshawo and Caowotan on the north. Covering an area of 682 square kilometers, Sitan features a terrain that is higher in the south and lower in the north, with an average altitude of 1,800 meters above sea level. The region enjoys an average annual temperature of 8.5 ℃, with an average annual sunshine duration of 2,713.5 hours and a frost-free period of 183 days. The average annual precipitation is approximately 180 mm, most of which occurs in July and August.

Sitan is divided into 15 administrative villages and 1 community with a registered population of 19,368. There are 248,000 *mu* of cultivated land. The special agricultural products include Heshangtou wheat flour, sunflower seeds and seed melons. In recent years, the planting area of seed melons has reached 24,500 *mu*. It has become a major cash crop that has significantly improved the livelihoods of local residents. The breeding industry relies mainly on raising pigs and sheep.

The town has convenient transportation with the Yingpanshui-Shuangta Expressway and National Highway 338 passing through, and is rich in mineral resources, including gypsum, coal and limestone. It also boasts many famous tourist attractions, such as the National Forest Park of Mount Shoulu, Yongtai Ancient Fort and Xindunwan Grassland, which attract numerous domestic and international tourists every year.

寺滩乡位于景泰西部，地处河西走廊东端，东临一条山镇、喜泉镇，南依寿鹿山、正路镇，西接古浪县、天祝县，北与上沙沃镇、草窝滩镇接界，总面积达到682平方千米。寺滩地势南高北低，平均海拔1800米，年平均气温8.5℃，年平均日照时数2713.5小时，无霜期183天，年降水量180毫米，主要集中在7、8月。

寺滩乡下辖15个行政村和1个社区，总户籍人口为19368人。全乡总耕地面积为24.8万亩，特色农产品包括和尚头面粉、葵花籽、籽瓜等。近年来，寺滩乡种植籽瓜面积达到2.45万亩，籽瓜已成为当地群众的"摇钱树"，助力他们迈向更美好的生活。养殖业以饲养猪、羊为主。

寺滩境内交通便利，营双高速、国道338穿境而过。这里矿产资源丰富，拥有石膏、煤炭、石灰石等。此外，寺滩乡旅游资源富集，拥有寿鹿山国家森林公园、永泰古城、新墩湾草原等众多著名旅游景点，每年吸引大量国内外的游客前来参观游览。

Yongtai Ancient Fort

13.11 Manshuitan 漫水滩乡

Manshuitan is located in the northwest of Jingtai and on the southern fringe of the Tengger Desert, with Alxa Left Banner on the east, Mount Changling on the west, Shangshawo on the south and Hongshui on the north. Historically, it was a vast wasteland. Every time there was a heavy rainstorm, mountain torrents from several Shahes would converge here, flooding the whole area. Thus it's called Manshuitan, which literally means "flat over-flowed by water".

Manshuitan covers an area of 170 square kilometers. The terrain is higher in the southwest and lower in the northeast, with an average altitude of 1,700 meters above sea level. Influenced by the desert climate, the town experiences frequent windy days and sandstorms hit the region from time to time. The average annual temperature is 6.5 ℃ and the annual rainfall is 210 mm, most of which occurs in August, September and October.

Manshuitan is divided into 11 administrative villages, with a registered population of 11,585. There are 68,700 *mu* of irrigated land. The main crops grown here include corn, wheat, onion and goji berries. The breeding industry focuses mainly on raising pigs, sheep and laying hens. The town is also rich in mineral resources, such as coal and limestone, which have contributed enormously to the region's economic development and provide a foundation for future growth.

漫水滩乡位于景泰县西北部，地处腾格里沙漠南缘，东接阿拉善左旗，西依长岭山，南邻上沙沃镇，北与红水镇接壤。漫水滩原是一片荒滩，每逢暴雨，多条山洪汇聚于此，洪水漫过这片荒滩，因而得名"漫水滩"。

漫水滩乡总面积为170平方千米，地势西南高而东北低，平均海拔

1700米。受沙漠气候的影响，该地区常遭遇大风天气和沙尘暴的侵袭，年平均气温为6.5 ℃，年降水量为210毫米，主要集中在8、9、10月份。

　　漫水滩乡现下辖11个行政村，总户籍人口为11585人。全乡拥有水浇地6.87万亩，种植业以玉米、小麦、洋葱、枸杞为主，畜牧业以生猪、羊、蛋鸡为主。此外，漫水滩乡还拥有丰富的矿产资源，主要包括煤炭、石灰石等。

Green Fields in Manshuitan